TABERNACLE
G*of*RACE

TABERNACLE
of
GRACE

Les Brittingham, B.S., M.Div.

TATE PUBLISHING
AND ENTERPRISES, LLC

Published by Tate Publishing & Enterprises, LLC
127 E. Trade Center Terrace | Mustang, Oklahoma 73064 USA
1.888.361.9473 | www.tatepublishing.com

Tate Publishing is committed to excellence in the publishing industry. The company reflects the philosophy established by the founders, based on Psalm 68:11,
"The Lord gave the word and great was the company of those who published it."

Book design copyright © 2016 by Tate Publishing, LLC. All rights reserved.
Cover design by Joana Quilantang
Interior design by Jomar Ouano

Published in the United States of America

ISBN: 978-1-68254-523-2
1. Religion / Christian Theology / Christology
2. Religion / Christian Rituals & Practice / Worship & Liturgy
15.12.04

About the Author

The founder of Manna Resource Institute, Les Brittingham, earned his BS at Corban University and his MDiv at Denver Baptist Theological Seminary, where he majored in biblical languages. Les is a Bible scholar who has taught in various academic and church settings for over twenty-five years and was a pastor in the Foursquare Denomination for fifteen years.

Bringing a rich academic and pastoral background to his books and seminars, Les has a sincere desire to equip believers in their understanding and presentation of God's Word.

He is available to speak to churches and other groups and lives in Fort Collins, Colorado, with his wife, Linda.

For other books written by the author, visit the Manna Resource Institute web site: www.mannari.com

If you would like more information on books and seminars or would like to learn more about the ministry of Les Brittingham and Manna Resource Institute, you can contact him by e-mail at lesbmri@q.com or call at 970-213-8158.

Other Books
Written by the Author

Taking a Second Look at the Second Coming
Decoding Daniel
Revelation Unraveled
Kingdom Combat
Christianity is a White Collar Job
The Amazing Secrets of the Zodiac
The Greek New Testament Made Easy (Two Volumes)
20 Keys to Effective Bible Study

Contents

PART V: THE HOLY PLACE

Introduction

Does God Have a Split Personality?

I remember the conversation as if it were yesterday. Before me was a torn and broken man. At one time, Bob had become a self-made millionaire in the mining business. Proud and powerful because of his success, no one could tell this man what to do with his life. However, after a bad turn of events, his fortune turned to rags, and he lost his money as fast as he gained it. Faced with his own mortality, he had more than one time put a gun to his head to end it all. His wife called and asked if I would meet with him.

Now it was time to talk about life and God. Bob was open to Christianity, and we discussed a whole range of religious issues. But one question he asked me still rings in my mind, as clear today as when he posed it several years ago. He inquired, "When I read the Bible, it seems to me that there are two gods. In the Old Testament, God appears to be cruel, vindictive, judgmental, and angry. In the New Testament, I see a God of love, mercy, and salvation. Which picture is correct?"

This is a fair question. There are many sincere people who have this same perception and confusion about God. It is hard to blame them. They read the Old Testament and are often treated to an array of brutal pictures of whole cities wiped out: men, women, and children. They often see vivid examples of judgment coming from the hand of God, and harsh words uttered by the Lord Himself. Then there are times when God exacts severe retribution as He did upon the world during Noah's time and against the cities of Sodom and Gomorrah. Contrast this with the New Testament Jesus—loving, healing, and embracing the lost with compassion and forgiveness. At face value, it does appear as if God went through a personality change from the Old Testament to the New Testament.

The Old Testament: A Place of Grace

Yes, there are harsh pictures of judgment in the Old Testament. But if one looks earnest enough, he will find numerous examples of God's grace and mercy as well. Adam and Eve should have immediately been punished by death for their brazen and blatant disobedience of the Lord's instruction in the Garden of Eden. Yet God, in mercy, spared them. When virtually the "whole" world had turned its back on the Lord in rebellion and opted for wickedness, He spared the human race from total destruction by saving Noah and his family from the flood.

We could speak of the Lord's mercy to Abraham, Isaac, Jacob, Aaron, David, and Jonah—men, who, at different points in their lives, sinned and disobeyed their God, yet were allowed to fulfill the destiny He had for them. It was God's grace that for over five hundred years, He put up with Israel's persistent disobedience, idolatry, obstinacy in the face of incessant warnings and wanton disregard for the covenant and law they had been given. Finally, His patience ran out, and judgment ensued, but His grace and long suffering had existed for a much longer period of time.

Then there are the pagan gentiles. The Lord reached out in mercy and touched them by bringing the revelation of Himself and allowing them to embrace Him: characters such as the harlot Rahab, a citizen from the pagan and godless city of Jericho; the Moabite Ruth from a heritage of people known for their defiance and hatred of Israel's God; and the healing of the Assyrian general Naaman, representing a nation whose sole purpose was to destroy Israel. Let's not forget the ruthless, boastful, and powerful Babylonian King Nebuchadnezzar, who, after witnessing incessant demonstrations of God's power and prescience, wrought, through the prophet Daniel, was forced to come off his perch of arrogance, acknowledging his fallibility and proclaiming the God of Israel as the true God.

It was to the wicked people in Nineveh, who practiced the most reprehensible and detestable lifestyles, that God commissioned the reluctant prophet Jonah to dissuade the people to turn from their wickedness and repent. After heeding the words of Jonah, the Lord relented and withdrew His hand of judgment. It was because of God's grace and mercy that Lot and his family were rescued from the wicked and vile cities of Sodom and Gomorrah. There are many more examples, but these illustrate the God of the Old Testament was not solely an executor of judgment but was truly compassionate, forgiving, and merciful.

A Picture is Worth a Thousand Words

Perhaps, the greatest example in the Old Testament regarding the Lord's grace and mercy was manifested in a simple tent called the *tabernacle*. Everything about it spoke of His compassion, love, and salvation destined to be fulfilled in the person of Christ. When one desires to describe something, he can choose to use many words and sentences to accomplish this. Or, to save time, he might point to an object and accomplish the same thing. As an illustration, if a young man desires to communicate to his parents what his new college girlfriend looks like, he can employ hundreds of words and sentences to describe her beauty, hair, eyes, and body shape. However, to save time and get his point across more quickly and poignantly, he could just say "she looks like Marilyn Monroe." If one wants to convey majesty, he can point to Mount Everest; or to express power, Niagara Falls.

In the same way, to communicate the grace, compassion, and mercy of God in the Old Testament, all that has to be mentioned is the word *tabernacle*. It is around this incredible tent edifice and symbol of grace in the Old Testament that we shall focus the rest of our discussion. I think you will come to agree with me this iconic symbol conveys the mercy and grace of God in a most powerful and dramatic way.

General Considerations

The study of the tabernacle is one of the most important topics a student of scripture can pursue in order to increase his knowledge and insight of the Word of God. Virtually, the entire Bible, in some way or another, references the tabernacle of the Old Testament. New Testament books such as Revelation and Hebrews are full of references to this unusual tent. The Apostle Paul often alluded to the tabernacle in his epistles, as well as did Peter and John. When one has a thorough knowledge and understanding of the tabernacle, he will be able to glean far more from the Word of God than he would otherwise. The following study is an attempt to discuss the tabernacle in a systematic and detailed fashion. We will look at all of its aspects, including the structure, furniture, priesthood, and the sacrifices. I trust that as we put this marvelous subject under the microscope of God's Spirit, we will be changed by the tabernacle's relevant salvation message for today in the person of Jesus Christ. Let our song truly be amazing grace!

A Type or Shadow of the Lord Jesus Christ

One of the most important principles we can discover in our approach to the Bible is that the Old Testament contains many types and shadows, which foreshadow the Lord Jesus Christ and His marvelous work of procuring salvation. The widely used adage "The New Testament is in the Old *concealed*, and the Old Testament is in the New *revealed*" is appropriate here. A *type* is simply a person, place, or event that points to something fulfilled in the future. This fulfillment is called the *antitype*. We find these Old Testament shadows completed in the New Testament. The New Testament frequently refers back to these types and their relationship to Christ. There are many types in the Old Testament that pointed to Jesus in the New Testament. For instance, the manna in the wilderness was fulfilled in Christ (John 6:32–35). The heart-wrenching scene, where Abraham attempts to sacrifice His son Isaac in Genesis 22, is all about prefiguring the relationship of God the Father to His Son Jesus who, one day, would be sacrificed according to His Father's plan. Jonah is a type of the resurrection of Christ, and the concept of the kinsman-redeemer found in the book of Ruth points to the redemption Jesus would enact for the church.

Scripture is unequivocal that the Old Testament pointed to Jesus (emphasis added):

> And beginning with Moses and all the Prophets, he explained to them what was said in all the *Scriptures concerning himself.* (Luke 24:27)

> You diligently study the Scriptures because you think that by them you possess eternal life. These are the Scriptures that *testify about me.* (John 5:39)

> Therefore do not let anyone judge you by what you eat or drink, or with regard to a religious festival, a New Moon celebration or a Sabbath day. These are a *shadow of the things that were to come; the reality, however, is found in Christ.* (Colossians 2:16–17)

> When Christ came as high priest of the good things that are already here, he went through the *greater and more perfect Tabernacle* that is not man-made, that is to say, not a part of this creation. (Hebrews 9:11)

> The law is only a *shadow* of the good things that are coming— not the realities themselves. For this reason it can never, by the same sacrifices repeated endlessly year after year, make perfect those who draw near to worship. (Hebrews 10:1)

The Gospel of John even identifies Jesus as a tent or tabernacle: "The Word *became* flesh and made his *dwelling [tabernacle]* among us. We have seen his glory, the glory of the One and Only, who came from the Father, full of *grace and truth*" (John 1:14; emphasis added).

The word for "made his dwelling" in John 1:14 is the Greek word for tent, *skēnoō*. This is a veiled reference to the tabernacle of the Old Testament. Just as the tabernacle contained the glory of God, Jesus, the fulfillment of the Old Testament picture through His incarnation, manifested the glory of God. The tabernacle in all of its components in some way pointed to Jesus Christ.

A Picture of the Church

The Old Testament is not only a picture and fulfillment of what would happen in Christ. It also foreshadows matters related to His church as well. It is interesting that the Apostle Paul refers to his own body as a tent: "Now we know that if the *earthly tent* we live in is destroyed, we have a building from God, an eternal house in heaven, not built by human hands" (2 Corinthians 5:1; emphasis added).

Jesus was the first human to fulfill the shadow of the Old Testament glory in His human tabernacle, and the church continues this pattern. We know from scripture that in God's people is where the glory of God dwells. Paul associates the glory of God with followers of Christ: "To them God has chosen to make known among the Gentiles the glorious riches of this mystery, which is *Christ in you*, the *hope of glory*. (Colossians 1:27; emphasis added).

There are other places in the New Testament where the church is referred to as a tent of God's origin and dwelling. In the book of Revelation, the church (God's bride) is referenced in this fashion (emphasis added):

> Therefore, "they are before the throne of God and serve him day and night in his temple; and he who sits on the throne will spread his *tent* over them. (Revelation 7:15)

> He opened his mouth to blaspheme God, and to slander his name and his *dwelling place* and those who live in heaven. (Revelation 13:6)

> I saw the Holy City, the New Jerusalem, coming down out of heaven from God, prepared as a *bride* beautifully dressed for her husband. And I heard a loud voice from the throne saying, "Now the *dwelling of God* is with men, and he will live with them. They will be his people, and God himself will be with them and be their God. (Revelation 21:2–3)

Whether in heaven or on the earth, the church is associated with the heavenly tent and the dwelling of God. These are beautiful pictures fulfilling Old Testament symbols. The Old Testament provides numerous shadows and types of the Lord Jesus as well as salvation. The biggest shadow is the tabernacle. Everything in it virtually points to Jesus and His work through the church.

The Place Where God Met Man

Christianity is unique among the religions of the world with its emphasis from the very beginning (Garden of Eden) on God's desire to have a personal relationship with mankind—His most treasured creation. The entire Bible is an unfolding story about God's passion to establish a *covenant* relationship with His people. From the creation of Adam to this day, God has always related Himself to humanity through a covenant. The tabernacle was truly an expressive arena in which a holy God met sinful mankind: "For the generations to come this burnt offering is to be made regularly at the entrance to the *Tent of Meeting* before the LORD. There *I will meet you* and speak to you" (Exodus 29:42; emphasis added).

Jesus Christ would later fulfill this picture in coming to earth to redeem mankind. *God* and *man* met in Him. Jesus was fully God and fully human. This meeting of divinity and humanity would play a key role in our salvation. The Bible is unequivocal in this regard (emphasis added):

> For God was pleased to have *all his fullness* dwell in him. (Colossians 1:19)

> Who, *being in very nature God*, did not consider equality with God something to be grasped, but made himself nothing, taking the very nature of a servant, *being made in human likeness*. (Philippians 2:6–7)

> The Son is the *radiance of God's glory* and the *exact representation of his being*, sustaining all things by his powerful word. After he had provided purification for sins, he sat down at the right hand of the Majesty in heaven. (Hebrews 1:3)

Christ, by His cross, would now provide the ultimate place where sinful mankind could meet a holy God in reconciliation. In the book of Second Corinthians, the Apostle Paul emphasizes this need for God and man to be reconciled:

> All this is from God, who reconciled us to himself through Christ and gave us the ministry of reconciliation: that *God was reconciling the world to himself* in Christ, not counting men's sins against them. And he has committed to us the message of reconciliation. We are therefore Christ's ambassadors, as though God were making his appeal through us. We implore you on Christ's behalf: Be reconciled to God. (2 Corinthians 5:18–20; emphasis added)

The Old Testament picture was temporary and incomplete. However, it would be a harbinger of a day when a greater tabernacle would emerge and provide a permanent way for man and God to be reconciled by the cross of Jesus Christ.

Originally God's Idea

Salvation never starts with man, but always with God. Rescuing and saving humanity was God's idea from the very beginning. After Adam and Eve sinned, it was the Lord who sought them out when they were hiding in fear and shame, and it was the Lord who provided the means of sacrifice for them to still live. When Paul was riding on the road to Damascus, consumed with vengeance and hate in his heart toward Christ and His followers, it was the Lord Jesus who dramatically struck him off his horse and sought him. It is no surprise then that the ultimate picture of salvation, the tabernacle, would originate in the heart and mind of God. All of these scriptures confirm this (emphasis added).

> Then have them make a sanctuary for me, and I will dwell among them. Make this Tabernacle and all its furnishings exactly like the pattern *I will show you.* (Exodus 25:8–9)

> Our forefathers had the Tabernacle of the Testimony with them in the desert. It had *been made as God directed* Moses, according to the pattern he had seen. (Acts 7:44)

> The point of what we are saying is this: We do have such a high priest, who sat down at the right hand of the throne of the Majesty in heaven, and who serves in the sanctuary, the true Tabernacle *set up by the Lord, not by man.* (Hebrews 8:1–2)

> They serve at a sanctuary that is a copy and shadow of what is in heaven. This is why Moses was warned when he was about to build the Tabernacle: "See to it that you make everything according to *the pattern shown you on the mountain.*" (Hebrews 8:5)

In fact, to further support this, in the tabernacle description of furniture in Exodus 25, the Lord starts with the Ark of the Covenant/Testimony located in the most holy place where He dwells and works backward to the bronze altar. Normally, one would think he would have started with the bronze altar at the entry point of the courtyard. This reversed approach illustrates salvation starts with Him: "Make this Tabernacle and all its furnishings exactly like the pattern I will show you. Have them make a chest of acacia wood—two and a half cubits long, a cubit and a half wide, and a cubit and a half high. Then put in the *ark the Testimony*, which I will give you" (Exodus 25:9–10, 16. emphasis added).

When it comes to sinful man, God is the one who seeks us first. Salvation always starts with Him, not us. Throughout the Bible, He is depicted as the one searching for the lost, not vice versa. In fact, Jesus indicates this in His comments to the disciples (emphasis added):

> For the Son of Man came *to seek* and to save what was lost. (Luke 19:10)

> You did not choose me, but *I chose you* and appointed you to go and bear fruit—fruit that will last. Then the Father will give you whatever you ask in my name. (John 15:16)

> No one can come to me unless the *Father who sent me draws him*, and I will raise him up at the last day. He went on to say, "This is why I told you that no one can come to me unless the Father has enabled him. (John 6:44–45)

Salvation commences with God. No human being can ever claim to have initiated it. We have always been the hunted and never the hunter. All we can do is stand in adoration, praise, and worship to God that He chose to pursue and love ungodly sinners such as us.

A Touch of *Grace* Following the Giving of the *Law*

It is worth noting that prior to the giving of the instructions for the tabernacle in Exodus 25–30, God had revealed His law to Israel in Exodus 20–24. The law was intended to show Israel His standards for their lives and was to be an expression of their love for Him. The Lord intended for Israel to live under a higher standard than the pagan nations around them. After the giving of the law, Israel responded in a positive and confident fashion: "Then he took the Book of the Covenant and read it to the people. They responded, '*We will do* everything the LORD has said; *we will obey*'" (Exodus 24:7; emphasis added).

Israel enthusiastically responded with a we-can-do attitude, fully persuaded they could pass the test. But God knew better, and in Exodus 25–31, He gave to Moses instructions for building the tabernacle. Even though the people were self-assured, they were capable of keeping the law; God foresaw they were destined to fail. It didn't take long to confirm Israel's weakness and propensity to sin by violating the Ten Commandments. In Exodus 32, we read that simultaneously as Moses was on the mountain with the Lord receiving the stone tablets of the law, Israel was sinning down below by building an idolatrous golden calf, which explicitly violated God's commandment against idolatry recorded in Exodus 20:22–26.

> Then the LORD said to Moses, "Tell the Israelites this: 'You have seen for yourselves that I have spoken to you from heaven: *Do not make any gods to be alongside me*; do not make for yourselves gods of silver or gods of gold. (Exodus 20:22–23; emphasis added)

> When the people saw that Moses was so long in coming down from the mountain, they gathered around Aaron and said, "Come, *make us gods* who will go before us. As for this fellow Moses who brought us up out of Egypt, we don't know what has happened to him." Aaron answered them, "Take off the gold earrings that your wives, your sons and your daughters are wearing, and bring them to me. So all the people took off their earrings and brought them to Aaron. He took what they handed him and *made it into an idol* cast in the shape of a calf, fashioning it with a tool. Then they said, "*These are your gods*, O Israel, who brought you up out of Egypt." Exodus 32:1–4; emphasis added)

After this brazen display of disobedience and the subsequent judgment that followed, instructions for the building of the tabernacle followed in the same way as they did in chapter 25. The instructions for the tabernacle are twice juxtaposed to matters relating to the law because grace would be needed after the failure of the people to obey the holy commandments. The New Testament overwhelmingly instructs us that the law condemned mankind and could never provide salvation (emphasis added):

> Therefore no one will be declared righteous in his sight by observing the law; rather, *through the law we become conscious of sin.* (Romans 3:20)

> Clearly *no one is justified before God by the law*, because, "The righteous will live by faith." (Galatians 3:11)

> He has made us competent as ministers of a new covenant— not of the letter but of the Spirit; for *the letter kills*, but the Spirit gives life. Now if the ministry that *brought death*, which was engraved in letters on stone, came with glory, so that the Israelites could not look steadily at the face of Moses because of its glory, fading though it was, will not the ministry of the Spirit be even more glorious? If the ministry that *condemns men* is glorious, how much more glorious is the ministry that brings righteousness! (2 Corinthians 3:6–9)

The whole tabernacle setup was a comprehensive description of God's grace offered to rescue a sinful people. Often, Bible readers find it difficult to see grace in the Old Testament. The tabernacle is the most emphatic statement of the mercy of God anywhere in scripture. In fact, the New Testament associates grace with the fulfillment of the tabernacle—Jesus Christ: "The *Word became flesh* and made his *dwelling* among us. We have seen his glory, the glory of the One and Only, who came from the Father, full of *grace* and truth" (John 1:14; emphasis added).

The New Testament expounds on this whole issue of grace seen so vividly in the Old Testament. Grace was the profound gift of God to sinners in both testaments: "For all have sinned and fall short of the glory of God, and are justified freely by his *grace* through the redemption that came by Christ Jesus" (Romans 3:23–24; emphasis added) and "For it is by *grace* you have been saved, through faith—

and this not from yourselves, it is the gift of God—not by works, so that no one can boast" (Ephesians 2:8–9; emphasis added).

Patterned After the Heavenly Tabernacle

We noted earlier that the impetus for building this tabernacle came from God, not man. The earthly tabernacle was patterned after a heavenly one, which is mentioned several times in scripture. God's heavenly tabernacle often interacts with God's people even to the present time.

Moses Shown the Heavenly Tabernacle

The book of Hebrews specifically tells us that the tabernacle of Moses was a copy of what was already in heaven. Moses was ordered to replicate what he saw: "They serve at a *sanctuary* that is a copy and *shadow of what is in heaven*. This is why Moses was warned when he was about to build the Tabernacle: 'See to it that you make everything according to the *pattern shown you* on the mountain'" (Hebrews 8:5; emphasis added).

Isaiah Saw the Heavenly Tabernacle

The prophet Isaiah was given the privilege of seeing the temple in the heavenly realm. Keep in mind that the temple was patterned after the tabernacle and virtually reflected the same structure and furniture setup. This is where the glory and presence of God was emphasized, "In the year that King Uzziah died, I saw the Lord seated on a throne, high and exalted, and the train of his robe filled the *temple*" (Isaiah 6:1; emphasis added).

Ezekiel Reveals the Heavenly Tabernacle

The prophet Ezekiel saw the throne and glory of God in connection with the divine-human figure: the son of man. Remember, the glory of God was originally found in the tabernacle, and later, the temple patterned after it.

Above the expanse over their heads was what looked like a *throne* of sapphire, and high above on the *throne* was a figure like that of a man. I saw that from what appeared to be his waist up he looked like glowing metal, as if full of fire, and that from there down he looked like fire; and brilliant light surrounded him. Like the appearance of a rainbow in the clouds on a rainy day, so was the radiance around him. This was the appearance of the likeness of the *glory of the* LORD. When I saw it, I fell facedown, and I heard the voice of one speaking. (Ezekiel 1:26–28; emphasis added)

Daniel References the Heavenly Tabernacle

Daniel was given an incredible view into the heavenly realm. Like Isaiah and Ezekiel, he saw the ancient of days seated on the throne of God. Remember, the earthly tabernacle and temple were where the presence of God was manifested on the earth. It was a replica of the heavenly throne scene: "As I looked, *thrones* were set in place, and the *Ancient of Days took his seat.* His clothing was as white as snow; the hair of his head was white like wool. His throne was flaming with fire, and its wheels were all ablaze" (Daniel 7:9; emphasis added).

John the Apostle Allowed to See the Heavenly Tabernacle

There is no greater expression of the tabernacle and temple in the heavens than the picture revealed to John the Apostle. John was given this insight to encourage his heart that there truly was a triumphal presence in the heavens, which influenced life on this planet. The following references to the throne, golden censer, incense, golden altar, and fire from the altar are unmistakable allusions and references to the Old Testament tabernacle, which Moses constructed (emphasis added):

At once I was in the Spirit, and there before me was a *throne in heaven* with someone sitting on it. And the one who sat there had the appearance of jasper and carnelian. A rainbow, resembling an emerald, encircled the throne. (Revelation 4:2–3)

Another angel, who had a *golden censer*, came and stood at the altar. He was given much *incense* to offer, with the prayers of all the saints, on the *golden altar* before the throne. The smoke of the incense, together with the prayers of the saints, went up before God from the angel's hand. Then the angel took the censer, filled it with *fire from the altar*, and hurled it on the earth; and there came peals of thunder, rumblings, flashes of lightning and an earthquake. (Revelation 8:3–5)

This heavenly tabernacle/temple is still operational today and has a great impact on the earth as believers touch God's presence with their worship and prayers.

The Tabernacle and Its Court

DISCUSSION QUESTIONS

1. Whose original idea was the tabernacle? What does this tell us about salvation?
2. What is the significance of the tabernacle instructions following the discussion of the law in Exodus? How does this apply to the believer's everyday life?
3. Relate the importance of the heavenly tabernacle/temple toward our understanding of God's working in our lives and on the earth today?
4. In what way is the church the tabernacle on earth? Why is it important to know this? How is this manifested on earth?

I

COMPOSITION
AND DESIGN

1

General Description

The tabernacle in its entirety pictured God's salvation plan through Christ. This included details of the general design and composition. The tabernacle, though powerful and anointed, was not an impressive building. This should come as no surprise as God's plan of salvation has rarely been associated with the spectacular.

A Simple Tent

It is important to note that the tabernacle wasn't a fancy edifice or a spectacular piece of architecture. The tabernacle was a simple tent. "Make curtains of goat hair for the *tent* over the Tabernacle—eleven altogether" (Exodus 26:7; emphasis added).

When we normally think of tents, we associate them with something that is not going to impress anyone. Tents are practical; designed to be carried on one's back; not fancy or gaudy; portable, not permanent; and generally, ordinary in color and design. Tents are composed of basic lightweight components designed to protect its inhabitants from the elements and most intrusive animals. Tents are intended to be practical, not palatial.

In the same way, salvation, reflected in the tabernacle, was not designed to emphasize outward splendor and beauty. It was truly functional and simple, not lavish or ostentatious. Ultimately, the pedestrian nature of this tent fit well with the ordinary and unpretentious nature of Jesus who was to come. Isaiah indicates there would be nothing spectacular in terms of the physical appearance of Jesus, the suffering servant: "He grew up before him like a tender shoot, and like a root out of dry ground. He had *no beauty or majesty* to attract us to him, nothing in his *appearance* that we should *desire* him" (Isaiah 53:2; emphasis added).

This does not imply that Jesus's face and body were ugly, repulsive, or hideous to behold. It simply means the main attraction about this man from Galilee was not His physical looks nor appearance. The Bible reveals that Jesus was indeed the fulfillment of this Old Testament symbol, the tabernacle. In the same way, there was nothing fancy or overly attractive about it. This was also true of Jesus: "The Word became flesh and made his *dwelling*, among us" (John 1:14; emphasis added).

The Tabernacle Composition

As we have stated, the tabernacle was a simple edifice. It was not complicated or intricate in its structure and composition. No scintillating embellishments like winding staircases, intriguing hallway passages, or multilevel floors filled with wondrous collections from around the world would describe this tent.

Three Basic Sections

The tabernacle consisted of three basic sections: the courtyard, the holy place, and the holy of holies. The last two sections comprised the main tent of tabernacle.

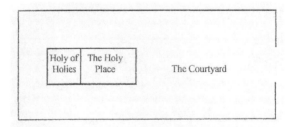

Some see an analogy to the human condition in these three compartments. Whereas the tabernacle was made up of three sections, human beings are also comprised of three parts: spirit, soul, and body. The outer court (or courtyard) compares with the human body: it's the place visible from the outside. The holy place relates to the soul: the seat of volition, thought, and emotion. The holy of holies is analogous to the human spirit, where the Holy Spirit lives. God's Spirit works in our spirit through the new birth to renew our soul so that we might glorify God in our bodies. Salvation affects all three areas of our being.

There are three words that describe how the tabernacle is a pattern for our Christian Life. The courtyard is the place of *preparation*. We must come by way of the cross and cleansing to enter the holy place, which is the place of *practice*. It is in the holy place that we serve and fellowship with the Lord while drawing the power and strength from His Holy Spirit to be His light to the world. This is also the place of prayer. This leads to the most holy place or holy of holies, which is the place of His *presence* and our worship and intimacy with Him.

The holy of holies represents the most personal aspects of our relationship to God. Full of the Holy Spirit, as we pray and fellowship with the Him in the holy place, we find ourselves becoming more intimate and personal with Him. God's presence is a powerful and renewing force in our lives. All of us need it, and the tabernacle is the greatest Old Testament symbol of how we can become close to the Lord by drawing near to Him. Though simple in structure, the tabernacle is dynamic in its effect.

Seven Pieces of Furniture

Not only was the tabernacle comprised of three sections. It also housed seven pieces of furniture. Seven in scripture is the perfect number, so the seven pieces of furniture paint a perfect picture of the plan of salvation found in Christ. We will discuss each piece in detail later, but here are the seven pieces: the bronze altar of sacrifice, the bronze basin, the golden candlestick, the table of bread, the altar of incense, the Ark of the Covenant, and the mercy seat. Each unit of furniture conveys a wonderful picture of the work of Christ.

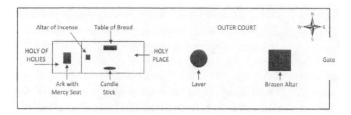

Constructed by Spirit-filled Workers

Everything in the tabernacle had a symbolic meaning, including those individuals who constructed it. These gifted craftsmen possessed special skills and had a specific anointing of God placed on them to complete their tasks. Scripture is very clear as to the identity of these workers and their relationship to the Holy Spirit (emphasis added):

> See, I have chosen *Bezalel son of Uri,* the son of Hur, of the tribe of Judah, and I have filled him with *the Spirit of God*, with skill, ability and knowledge in all kinds of crafts. (Exodus 31:2–3)

> Moreover, I have appointed *Oholiab son of Ahisamach*, of the tribe of Dan, to help him. Also *I have given skill* to all the craftsmen to make everything I have commanded you. (Exodus 31:6)

Two spirit-filled men primarily did the construction of the tabernacle. Their names reflective of the symbolism of the tabernacle: Bezalel, whose name means *in the shadow of God*, and Oholiab, whose name embodies the idea of *tent of my father*. The tabernacle was a tent designed and implemented by God. Much like the composition of Holy Scripture (2 Peter 1:21), it was a collaboration between human beings and the Spirit of God. It also was a shadow of God's plan for salvation. This is a picture and portend of our salvation, which could not happen apart from the work of the Holy Spirit (emphasis added).

> Jesus answered, "I tell you the truth, no one can enter the kingdom of God unless he is *born of water and the Spirit.* Flesh gives birth to flesh, but the *Spirit gives birth* to spirit." (John 3:5–6)

> He saved us, not because of righteous things we had done, but because of his mercy. *He saved us* through the washing of rebirth and renewal by the *Holy Spirit.* (Titus 3:5)

A Mobile Structure

God desired His tent and glory to be mobile. He didn't want Israel to become comfortable in any one spot. They were to follow the Lord wherever and whenever He led them. The instructions were clear and definitive in this regard.

> At the Lord's command the Israelites set out, and at his command they encamped. As long as the cloud stayed over the Tabernacle, they remained in camp. When the cloud remained over the Tabernacle a long time, the Israelites obeyed the Lord's order and did not set out. *Sometimes the cloud was over the Tabernacle only a few days*; at the Lord's command they would encamp, and then at his command *they would set out.* Sometimes the cloud stayed only from evening till morning, and when it lifted in the morning, *they set out.* Whether by day or by night, whenever the cloud lifted, *they set out.* Whether the cloud stayed over the Tabernacle for two days or a month or a year, the Israelites would remain in camp and not set out; but when it lifted, *they would set out. At the Lord's command they encamped, and at the Lord's command they set out.* They obeyed the Lord's order, in accordance with his command through Moses. (Numbers 9:18–23; emphasis added)

In keeping with the symbol and typology of the tabernacle as a picture of salvation, the mobile nature of this edifice depicts salvation as a journey and a process in following God. We need His mercy and grace in this walk we call the Christian life. Also, this illustrates God's desire that we not become comfortable in any one place but be willing to follow Him into situations that stretch us beyond our comfort zones. In addition, salvation is pictured here as something to be carried to different places. The message of the gospel goes on and on as followers of Christ travel throughout the earth. Jesus exhorted His disciples to carry His salvation to the world (emphasis added):

> Therefore *go* and make disciples of *all nations*, baptizing them in the name of the Father and of the Son and of the Holy Spirit, and teaching them to obey everything I have commanded you. And surely I am with you always, to the very end of the age. (Matthew 28:19–20)

> He said to them, "*Go into all the world* and preach the good news to all creation." (Mark 16:15)

Two Tabernacles

Apparently, there were two tabernacles in the Old Testament: the initial tabernacle of Moses and the ensuing one of David.

Moses's Tabernacle

Moses's original tabernacle was located in Shiloh where the Ark of the Covenant was kept.

> When the soldiers returned to camp, the elders of Israel asked, "Why did the Lord bring defeat upon us today before the Philistines? Let us bring the ark of the Lord's covenant from *Shiloh*, so that it may go with us and save us from the hand of our enemies." So the people sent men to Shiloh, and they brought back the Ark of the Covenant of the Lord Almighty, who is enthroned between the cherubim. And

Eli's two sons, Hophni and Phinehas, were there with the *Ark of the Covenant of God*. (1 Samuel 4:3–4; emphasis added)

Eventually, at Shiloh, the Ark of the Covenant (the most precious item of furniture in the tabernacle) fell into the enemy hands of the Philistines because of the wickedness of Israel's leadership. This was a dark and foreboding time in the life of Israel. But hope was coming in the reign of Kind David.

David's Tabernacle

Eventually, David realized that, after many years away from Israel's camp, the glory of God associated with the Ark of the Covenant needed to be back with Israel where it belonged. He went and retrieved it, reestablishing the tabernacle as a center of spiritual operation. David's tabernacle was much more open and personal than that of Moses. This fact was reflected in the music and worship associated with it.

These are the men David put in charge of the music in the house of the LORD after the ark came to rest there. They *ministered with music before the Tabernacle*, the Tent of Meeting, until Solomon built the temple of the LORD in Jerusalem. They performed their duties according to the regulations laid down for them. (1 Chronicles 6:31–32; emphasis added)

David's reign brought back the glory and power of Israel's God but eventually, the people became disobedient again, bringing the Old Testament to a sad end. However, with a message of hope, the prophet Amos foresaw the restoration of David's tabernacle in the future: "In that day I will *restore David's fallen tent*. I will repair its broken places, restore its ruins, and build it as it used to be, so that they may possess the remnant of Edom and all the nations that bear my name," declares the LORD, who will do these things" (Amos 9:11–12; emphasis added)

The prophet Amos spoke of a day when the glory of David's tabernacle would reemerge in a powerful way. The New Testament interprets this day as the day of Jesus Christ's work on the earth,

> Simon has described to us how God at first showed his concern by taking from the Gentiles a people for himself. The words of the prophets are in agreement with this, as it is written: "After this, *I will return and rebuild David's fallen tent*. Its ruins I will rebuild, and I will restore it, that the remnant of men may seek the Lord, and all the Gentiles who bear my name", says the Lord, who does these things. (Acts 15:14–17; emphasis added)

David's tabernacle, with its focus on intimacy and worship, demonstrated dramatically that God wanted a personal relationship with His people. The final manifestation of the restoration of David's tabernacle would need to wait for the coming of Christ.

DISCUSSION QUESTIONS

1. What is the importance of the tabernacle being an ordinary tent? What is the application for us today?
2. How does the role the Holy Spirit played in the construction of the tabernacle relate to our salvation? How is this lived out practically?
3. What was so unique about the tabernacle of David? Discuss the application of this for the church today. How important is worship in our relationship with God?

II

An Outer Look

2

Outside the Tabernacle

Remember that the tabernacle is a picture of Christ and salvation. No detail is wasted in the symbolism. Even the items on the outside of the main fence of the tabernacle convey important principles rich in symbolism.

The Tribal Placements

There were twelve tribes in Israel. Each tribal name was a symbol of Christ. Three tribes were situated on each side of the outer fence. However, the way the tribes were designated to position themselves around the tabernacle, as presented in chapter 2 of the book of Numbers, was also important. We have highlighted the first tribe mentioned for each direction and its significant symbol of Christ:

Eastside: *Judah*, Issachar, Zebulun (Numbers 2:3–7)

Judah's symbol was a lion, king of the beasts. The lion represents Jesus as the King. Jesus was from the tribe of Judah so it was fitting that this tribe be positioned at the entry point. We enter God's salvation through Jesus the King (Gospel of Matthew).

West Side: *Ephraim*, Manasseh, Benjamin (Numbers 2:18–24)

Ephraim's symbol was an ox, an animal of labor and work. The ox depicts Jesus as the servant. Jesus laid His life down as a servant (Gospel of Mark).

South Side: *Reuben*, Simeon, Gad (Numbers 2:10–16)

The symbol of Reuben was a man. The man relates to Jesus's humanity. Jesus was the perfect man so He could represent mankind on the cross (Gospel of Luke).

North Side: *Dan*, Asher, Naphtali (Numbers 2:25–31)

The symbol of Dan was an eagle, which speaks of majesty and regal stature in the skies. The eagle represents Jesus's deity (Gospel of John).

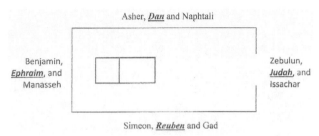

Asher, *Dan* and Naphtali

Benjamin, *Ephraim*, and Manasseh

Zebulun, *Judah*, and Issachar

Simeon, *Reuben* and Gad

The tribal positions all symbolized the Lord Jesus Christ. Not only were the tribal placements significant, but the high priest's position was important as well.

The Priest's Encampment

The high priest and his family were positioned on the eastside of the tabernacle in front of the east gate, the only entry point from the outside. "Moses and *Aaron and his sons* were to camp to the *east* of the Tabernacle, toward the sunrise, in front of the Tent of Meeting. They were responsible for the care of the sanctuary on behalf of the Israelites. Anyone else who approached the sanctuary was to be put to death" (Numbers 3:38; emphasis added).

Again, this position of the high priest near the entrance symbolizes that one cannot enter the tabernacle unless he comes through the high priest. This would later be fulfilled by Jesus Christ, who became our High Priest so that we could participate in God's salvation. "Therefore, since we have a great *high priest* who has gone through the heavens, Jesus the Son of God, let us hold firmly to the faith we profess" (Hebrews 4:14; emphasis added).

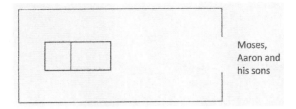

Moses, Aaron and his sons

The Perimeter Fence

The outer fence was strategic and embodied rich symbolism. It was what one viewed from the outside of the tabernacle and conveyed a powerful message. Each part of the fence is symbolic of Christ in some way.

Linen Curtains Surrounded the Courtyard

In Exodus 27:18, we are told that the curtains around the courtyard were made of fine linen. This linen was a very delicate white material. It symbolized purity and demonstrated to all who saw it that one had to be pure to enjoy God's salvation. Also, since there was only one entry point into the courtyard, this fence was symbolic of man's sinfulness and inability to get into the tabernacle on his own merit. "The courtyard shall be a hundred cubits long and fifty cubits wide, with *curtains of finely twisted linen* five cubits high, and with bronze bases" (Exodus 27:18; emphasis added).

Silver Hooks, Bands Held Up the Curtains

The hooks and the bands holding the linen curtains in place were made of silver (the tops on the post were overlaid with silver as well). Silver was a very important metal used in the tabernacle because it pointed to mankind's need of redemption. We will elaborate on the details of this point later when we come to the discussion of the redemption money.

> The north side shall also be a hundred cubits long and is to have curtains, with twenty posts and twenty bronze bases and with *silver hooks and bands* on the posts. (Exodus 27:11; emphasis added)

The hooks and bands on the posts were silver, and their *tops were overlaid with silver*, so all the posts of the courtyard had silver bands. (Exodus 38:17; emphasis added)

Bronze Bases Provided the Foundation. Tent Pegs Were Bronze As Well

The bases providing the foundation for the courtyard fence were constituted of bronze. We are not told what the poles were constructed of, but they were most likely comprised of acacia wood. Scripture also states the tent pegs used for the courtyard fence, as well as those used in the tabernacle itself, were bronze. Bronze in the Old Testament was a symbol of judgment. This will be discussed in more detail under our discussion of the altar of burnt offering. Everyone beholding the tabernacle from the outside was receiving the message that he was under a sentence of judgment because of his sin. "The north side shall also be a hundred cubits long and is to have curtains, with twenty *posts* and twenty *bronze bases*" (Exodus 27:11; emphasis added) and "All the *tent pegs* of the tabernacle and of the surrounding courtyard were *bronze*" (Exodus 38:20; emphasis added).

The East Gate

The east gate, which provided the entry point to the courtyard, is rich with symbolism regarding Christ and salvation.

There Was Only One Gate

"On the *east end*, toward the sunrise, the courtyard shall also be fifty cubits wide. Curtains fifteen cubits long are to be on *one side of the entrance*, with three posts and three bases, and curtains fifteen cubits long are to be on the other side, with three posts and three bases" (Exodus 27:13–15; emphasis added).

The only way one could enter the tabernacle was through the east gate. This gate is placed there by design, as it also depicts and foreshadows Jesus Christ, since He is described in the New

Testament as the only gate whereby one can enter salvation. "Therefore Jesus said again, 'I tell you the truth, *I am the gate* for the sheep'" (John 10:7; emphasis added).

He is the one true gate. The Greek construction for the translation *I am* is *ego eimi*, an intensive form of the personal pronoun, which could be translated, *I and only I*. Jesus is the only gate into salvation, there is no other. We live in a time when the idea that all roads lead to God is fashionable and popular in our modern culture. However, Jesus made it clear that He is the only gate for the sheep to find salvation, and He is the only way to the Father: "Jesus answered, "*I am the way* and the truth and the life. No one comes to the Father *except through me*" (John 14:6; emphasis added).

This is confirmed in the New Testament as well. "*Salvation is found in no one else*, for there is no other name under heaven given to men by which we must be saved" (Acts 4:12).

The Gate's Curtain was Special as Well.

There were four primary colors in the gate's curtain. "For the entrance to the courtyard, provide curtain twenty cubits long, of *blue, purple* and *scarlet* yarn and finely twisted *linen*—the work of an embroiderer—with four posts and four bases. All the posts around the courtyard are to have silver bands and hooks, and bronze bases" (Exodus 27:16–17; emphasis added).

Each of the colors in the curtain symbolized Christ in some way.

- Purple.Royalty: Jesus the King (Gospel of Matthew)
- Red.Blood: Jesus the suffering servant (Gospel of Mark)
- White.Purity: Jesus the perfect man (Gospel of Luke)
- Blue.Heaven: Jesus the Son of God (Gospel of John)

The fence around the tabernacle, the curtains, and the gate all poignantly portray the fact that man cannot come into God's presence and service any way that he wishes. He must enter by the Lord Jesus Christ. His sin and God's holy demands make it impossible for man to achieve salvation on his own. He must enter through the blood of Christ. "Therefore, brothers, since we have confidence to enter the Most Holy Place *by the blood of Jesus*" (Hebrews 10:19; emphasis added).

DISCUSSION QUESTIONS

1. Why was there only one entrance into the tabernacle, and why was the high priest encamped in front of the gate? What did the gate ultimately picture? How does this relate to the message of salvation we preach to the world?
2. What message was the outer fence sending to all who were looking at it from the outside? How does that message relate to the world today?
3. Discuss the significance of the colors on the gate curtain. How do they relate to the four Gospels? What do they tell us about Jesus?
4. How would you use the teaching on the gate to respond to someone who espouses the view that there is more than one way to have a relationship with God?

III

THE COURTYARD

3

The Bronze Altar

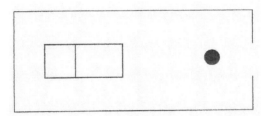

The courtyard was located outside of the holy place and the main structure of the tabernacle proper (main tent). Obviously, one could not enter the holy place until he had come through the outer court. All of the items in the outer court prepared one for participation in the holy place. The first object and the largest piece of furniture one encountered when he came into the courtyard was the bronze altar or the altar of sacrifice. The bronze altar is a powerful picture of the Lord Jesus Christ and frames the initial steps required for salvation.

> *Build an altar of acacia wood*, three cubits high; it is to be square, five cubits long and five cubits wide. Make a horn at each of the four corners, so that the horns and the altar are of one piece, and *overlay the altar with bronze.* Make all its *utensils of bronze*—its pots to remove the ashes, and its shovels, sprinkling bowls, meat forks and firepans. Make a grating for it, a bronze network, and make a bronze ring at each of the four corners of the network. Put it under the ledge of the altar so that it is halfway up the altar. Make poles of acacia wood for the altar and overlay them with bronze. The poles are to be inserted into the rings so they will be on two sides of the altar when it is carried. Make the

altar hollow, out of boards. It is to be made just as you were shown on the mountain. (Exodus 27:1–8; emphasis added)

The Starting Point for Salvation

Salvation starts with sacrifice. We cannot enter into the holy place or the holy of holies unless we first approach the altar of sacrifice. Adam and Eve, after their fall in the Garden of Eden, were the first people to experience the necessity of animal sacrifice and the shedding of blood to save them from judgment. We read in Genesis that they were wearing the skins of animals, implying that blood had been shed: "The LORD God made *garments of skin* for Adam and his wife and clothed them" (Genesis 3:21; emphasis added).

This practice would be continued in the tabernacle and, later, the temple. The altar and sacrifices all pictured and foreshadowed the ultimate sacrifice of the Lord Jesus Christ. Blood must be shed if a sacrifice is to be effective. "In fact, the law requires that nearly everything be cleansed with *blood*, and *without the shedding of blood there is no forgiveness*" (Hebrews 9:22; emphasis added).

Made of Acacia Wood

The altar was constructed of acacia wood, a species of the Shitta tree. "Build an altar of *acacia wood*, three cubits high; it is to be square, five cubits long and five cubits wide" Exodus 27:1; emphasis added).

This wood was used in many of the pieces of furniture in the tabernacle. Because it grew in harsh, arid conditions, it was well-suited for the desert and the nomadic nature of the tabernacle. This was a very hard, heavy, and enduring wood known for its indestructible nature and resistance to the destruction by insects. Symbolically, this hardy wood represented the enduring humanity of Jesus, who would also be reared in difficult times and experience great persecution and trial during His lifetime, only to be raised from the dead to live forever. In fact, in Isaiah 53:2, the prophet describes Jesus as one who grew up like a root out of dry ground. Today, Jesus still lives as a human being. We normally don't think of

Jesus in this way, but He is still the God-man in heaven. Jesus was the first human being to enter heaven, and He paved the way for us. "Therefore, since we have a great high priest who has *gone through the heavens*, Jesus the Son of God, let us hold firmly to the faith we profess" (Hebrews 4:14; emphasis added)

Covered in Bronze

God's instructions were very specific that the altar, as well as the utensils used in association with it, were to be overlaid with bronze. "Make a horn at each of the four corners, so that the horns and the altar are of one piece, and *overlay the altar with bronze*. Make all its *utensils of bronze*—its pots to remove the ashes, and its shovels, sprinkling bowls, meat forks and firepans" (Exodus 27:2–3; emphasis added).

As we have noted before, bronze is the symbol of judgment in the Old Testament, and it could withstand the intense heat placed upon it. There is another place in the Old Testament where bronze is associated with a form of judgment and, at the same time, spoke of relief from that judgment. After God severely judged Israel in the Old Testament for her sins by sending venomous snakes to bite them (Numbers 21:6), He had Moses make a bronze snake, which symbolized judgment. Yet it also provided a pathway for restoration. This also foreshadowed the cross of Christ: "So Moses made a *bronze snake* and put it up on a pole. Then when anyone was bitten by a snake and looked at the bronze snake, *he lived*" (Numbers 21:9; emphasis added) and "Just as *Moses lifted up the snake* in the desert, so the Son of Man must be lifted up, that everyone who believes in him may have eternal life" (John 3:14–15; emphasis added).

Sins were judged on the bronze altar with the sacrifice of the animals, just as our sins were placed on Jesus's body on the cross as a judgment. It is important to note that the bronze took the shape of the wood that framed the altar, symbolizing that, in the future, our judgment would be placed on an altar shaped as a human being: Jesus Christ.

But he was *pierced for our transgressions*, he was *crushed for our iniquities*; the *punishment* that brought us peace was upon him, and by his *wounds* we are healed. We all, like sheep, have gone astray, each of us has turned to his own way; and the LORD has laid on him the iniquity of us all. (Isaiah 53:5–6; emphasis added)

He himself *bore our sins in his body* on the tree, so that we might die to sins and live for righteousness; by his wounds you have been healed. (1 Peter 2:24; emphasis added)

A Place of Animal Sacrifice

The bronze altar was the first piece of furniture one encountered in the courtyard, symbolizing that salvation starts with sacrifice—the sacrifice of animals. "Then Aaron's sons the priests shall *arrange the pieces*, including the head and the fat, on the burning wood that is on the altar" (Leviticus 1:8).

All sacrifices placed on this altar would point to the future sacrifice of the Lord Jesus Christ. Christ was our sacrifice and the substitute for our sins. After the crucifixion of Christ, there would never be a need for another sacrifice to deal with the sins of mankind. Scripture supports this point (emphasis added).

The next day John saw Jesus coming toward him and said, "Look, *the Lamb of God*, who *takes away the sin* of the world! (John 1:29)

God made him who had no sin *to be sin for us*, so that in him we might become the righteousness of God. (2 Corinthians 5:21)

The blood of goats and bulls and the ashes of a heifer sprinkled on those who are ceremonially unclean sanctify them so that they are outwardly clean. How much more, then, *will the blood of Christ*, who through the eternal Spirit offered himself unblemished to God, cleanse our consciences from acts that lead to death, so that we may serve the living God! (Hebrews 9:13–14)

Because *it is impossible for the blood of bulls and goats to take away sins*. Therefore, when *Christ came* into the world, he said: "Sacrifice and offering you did not desire, but a body you prepared for me" (Hebrews 10:4–5)

Associated with Fire

Fire was continually represented on the bronze altar. It was a symbol of God's presence and His judgment and holiness. We can see it vividly and dramatically associated with Mount Sinai: "Mount Sinai was covered with smoke, because *the* Lord *descended on it in fire*. The smoke billowed up from it like smoke from a furnace, the whole mountain trembled violently" (Exodus 19:18; emphasis added).

There were two very important aspects of the fire in connection with the altar.

The Fire Originated with God

Fire on the altar originated from the Lord. No other source was allowed. When the fire of God fell on the altar, it was an indication that judgment for sin had been transferred to the animal and taken away from the people. An acceptable sacrifice always brought great joy. "*Fire came out from the presence of the* Lord and consumed the burnt offering and the fat portions on the altar. And when all the people saw it, they shouted for joy and fell facedown" (Leviticus 9:24).

In the New Testament, God is still a consuming fire as He responds to acceptable sacrifices of the New Testament priesthood. "Therefore, since we are receiving a kingdom that cannot be shaken, let us be thankful, and so worship God *acceptably* with reverence and awe, for our 'God is *a consuming fire*'" (Hebrews 12:28–29; emphasis added).

The Fire Was to Burn Perpetually

The fire was symbolic of God's judgment and presence. Fire was to incessantly burn on the altar, reminding the Jews that God's wrath must always be appeased. "*The fire on the altar must be kept burning; it must not go out.* Every morning the priest is to add firewood and arrange the burnt offering on the fire and burn the fat of the fellowship offerings on it. The fire must be kept burning on the altar *continuously*; it must not go out" (Leviticus 6:12–13; emphasis added).

The constant offering of sacrifices and the continual burning of fire reminded the people of the perpetual nature of their sins and the ongoing need for forgiveness. Later, a sacrifice in the person of Christ would appease God's wrath forever. "For God did not *appoint us to suffer wrath* but to receive salvation through our Lord Jesus Christ" (1 Thessalonians 5:9; emphasis added).

Four Horns Around the Altar

"*Make a horn at each of the four corners*, so that the horns and the altar are of one piece, and overlay the altar with bronze" (Exodus 27:2; emphasis added).

Horns in scripture symbolize power. In fact, Daniel 7:24 references the *ten horns* as the ten powerful kings who would come in the future. The number four is often associated with the earth. We often use the phrase *the four corners of the earth*. Here, the horns represent the power of salvation as it goes throughout the earth. Paul references this idea in his letters (emphasis added): "For the message of the cross is foolishness to those who are perishing, but to us who are being saved it is *the power of God*" (1 Corinthians 1:18) and "I am not ashamed of the gospel, because it is the *power of God* for the salvation of *everyone who believes*: first for the Jew, then for the Gentile" (Romans 1:16).

Transported by Priests

One of the unique features of the bronze altar was that it was to be transported on poles by priests, the spiritual leadership of Israel. "Make *poles of acacia wood* for the altar and overlay them with bronze. The poles are to be inserted into the rings so they will be on two sides of the altar when *it is carried*" (Exodus 27:6–7; emphasis added).

The priests carrying the altar symbolized the fact that we, the New Testament priesthood (1 Peter 2:9), carry the gospel and the cross of Christ wherever we go. We herald the message to the world that Jesus, through His sacrifice, has paid for their sin. The New Testament is unanimous in this declaration (emphasis added):

> Therefore go and make disciples of *all nations*, baptizing them in the name of the Father and of the Son and of the Holy Spirit. (Matthew 28:19)

> We are therefore *Christ's ambassadors*, as though God was making his appeal through us. We implore you on Christ's behalf: be reconciled to God. God made him who had no sin to be sin for us, so that in him we might become the righteousness of God. (2 Corinthians 5:20–21)

Every part of this altar proclaimed some aspect of the death of Christ. It is the starting point toward salvation and a relationship with God. Everything of spiritual significance that follows in the rest of the tabernacle depends on the cross and the sacrifice placed upon it.

The Brazen Altar

DISCUSSION QUESTIONS

1. Why is the bronze altar the first piece of furniture encountered in the courtyard?
2. What is bronze symbolic of in the Bible? How does this relate to the altar and to our salvation?
3. What did the acacia wood represent? Why is this important for the church today?
4. How can the New Testament church communicate the judgment of God in a positive way to the world she is trying to reach?

4

THE BRONZE BASIN

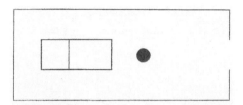

After one encountered the bronze altar in the courtyard, he then came to the bronze basin or laver.

> Make a *Bronze Basin*, with its bronze stand, for washing. Place it between the Tent of Meeting and the altar, and put water in it. Aaron and his sons are to wash their hands and feet with water from it. Whenever they enter the Tent of Meeting, they shall wash with water so that they will not die. Also, when they approach the altar to minister by presenting an offering made to the LORD by fire, they shall wash their hands and feet so that they will not die. This is to be a lasting ordinance for Aaron and his descendants for the generations to come. (Exodus 30:18–21; emphasis added)

Remember, the tabernacle had a dirt floor, so the priests were constantly washing themselves because their feet were always in contact with the earth. The basin not only represented their need to be cleansed physically but, symbolically, depicted their need to be cleansed spiritually. In fact the priests, like all of us, were sinners. Scripture teaches us that Jesus, our High Priest, was the only priest who did not need cleansing for sins.

> Such a high priest meets our need—one who is holy, blameless, pure, set apart from sinners, exalted above the heavens. *Unlike the other high priests, he does not need to offer sacrifices day after day, first for his own sins,* and then for the sins of the people. He sacrificed for their sins once for all when he offered himself. (Hebrews 7:26–27; emphasis added)

The basin also pointed to cleansing every believer needs in his daily life. Here are some of the symbolic features of the basin.

Made from Bronze Mirrors

The basin was made from the bronze mirrors used by the ladies. "They made the Bronze Basin and its bronze stand from the *mirrors of the women* who served at the entrance to the Tent of Meeting" (Exodus 38:8; emphasis added).

In a sense, mirrors can represent a mild form of vanity, since we are prone to preen and admire ourselves in them. Symbolically, God was asking the women to trade their vanity for purity and cleansing. Again, bronze used in the tabernacle symbolizes that all cleansing is the result of sacrifice and judgment previously enacted on the bronze altar. Our cleansing is based on the cross of Christ.

No Dimensions

The basin is the only piece of furniture in the tabernacle with no specified dimensions. This fact speaks of the unlimited forgiveness of the Lord regarding our sin and filth. The Bible underscores this idea in the New Testament. "If we confess our sins, he is faithful and just and will *forgive us our sins* and purify us from *all unrighteousness*" (1 John 1:9; emphasis added).

God's forgiveness has no size or shape. It can be as big or as small as we need. Perhaps this is what Paul meant when he described God's love by placing on it no dimensional limits: "So that Christ may dwell in your hearts through faith. And I pray that you, being rooted and established in love, may have power, together with all the saints, *to grasp how wide and long and high and deep is the love of Christ*" (Ephesians 3:17–18; emphasis added).

A Symbol of Daily Cleansing

This basin was required for the priest to wash his hands and feet, not necessarily his whole body. This is important in the symbolism: "Aaron and his sons are to wash their *hands and feet* with water from it" (Exodus 30:19; emphasis added).

Whereas the bronze altar of sacrifice represented the need for total cleansing, the bronze basin pictured that once our sins have been forgiven at the cross, we need continual cleansing of the little sins that occur daily in our lives. Jesus communicated this point at the last supper He had with His disciples by emphasizing their feet. Jesus answered, "A person who has had a *bath* needs only to *wash his feet*; his whole body is clean. And you are clean, though not every one of you" (John 13:10; emphasis added).

Two Greek words used in this passage represent cleansing. The first one translated bath is *bathos*. This word means *total and complete washing* and is what happened when one came to the bronze altar; he in essence received a complete spiritual bath. He was totally cleansed of all sin. This is analogous to when we initially accept Christ to receive salvation and establish a relationship with

God. The second word translated wash is *niptō,* and it stresses the daily cleansing of sin symbolized by the bronze basin. The believer does not need a complete bath or to be saved all over again. This daily cleansing of sin emphasized by the use of "feet" in the text speaks of the need to restore our fellowship with God, since we already have a relationship with Him. It is interesting to note that the symbolism of daily cleansing is spoken of by John in his first letter chapter 1 verse 9.

The water in the basin may also symbolize the Word of God. Scripture teaches us that the Word washes us: "How can a young man keep his way *pure?* By living according to your *word"* (Psalm 119:9; emphasis added) and "To make her holy, cleansing her by the washing with water through the word" (Ephesians 5:26).

The Word of God is the basin we wash in to keep ourselves pure in our walk.

The Last Stop on the Way to the Holy Place

The bronze basin was the last piece of furniture one encountered before he entered the worship center or the tabernacle tent itself. It is important to see the symbolism here. Cleansing is an essential priority for service and worship. David cried: "*Create in me a pure heart,* O God, and renew a steadfast spirit within me" (Psalm 51:10; emphasis added).

Jesus said this about worship and its relationship to holiness and character: "God is spirit, and his worshipers must *worship in spirit and in truth"* (John 4:24; emphasis added).

The bronze basin is strategically juxtaposed next to the holy place where the priests served and ministered to the Lord. The priests were continually balancing cleansing along with their priestly duties. In the same way, it is important that we keep our lives cleansed and pure as we prepare to worship and serve our God. We do this cleansing by confession. "If we *confess our sins,* he is faithful and just and will forgive us our sins and purify us from all unrighteousness" (1 John 1:9). ·

The word *confession* is *homologeō*, which means to *say the same thing*. God desires that we agree with him that our actions and behavior of sin are wrong and need to be confessed in a spirit of repentance and contrition. God will forgive and cleanse us of our sins if we will come to Him with sincere hearts and ask forgiveness. Participation in the bronze basin was a necessary prelude before the priests could perform their sacred service unto the Lord in the holy place.

The Laver of Brass

DISCUSSION QUESTIONS

1. What application is there in the fact that the basin lacked dimensions? What does this reveal about the love of God?
2. How does 1 John 1:9 typify the bronze basin?
3. Why was it necessary for the bronze basin to be the last stop before one entered the holy place? What does this say about God's viewpoint of holiness and worship?
4. How did Jesus's instructions in John 13:6–12 illustrate the meaning of the bronze basin?

IV

The Tabernacle Proper

5

The Main Tent

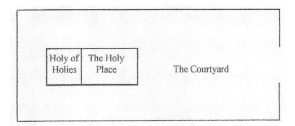

When we refer to the tabernacle in general, we usually mean the whole setup from the courtyard to the holy of holies. However, the tabernacle proper was more specifically the main tent itself. This was the true tabernacle where the priests served and God's glory resided. Everything discussed to this point has led to the tabernacle proper. Like the outer fence and the courtyard furniture, each detail in the tent construction conveyed a symbolic meaning and purpose. All of it pointed in some way or another to the Lord Jesus and the salvation He provided.

Special Frames for Support

The frames were the supports around the tent, which provided its structure. The Lord gave two basic instructions for the construction of the frames.

Constructed of Acacia Wood

"Make upright frames of *acacia wood* for the Tabernacle" (Exodus 26:15; emphasis added).

As you recall, acacia wood was a very durable type of wood. It typifies the humanity of Jesus, which continues on forever. Without the frames, the tent could not have functioned as a picture of God's salvation plan, nor could it have lasted through the harsh weather in the desert conditions of the wilderness. Likewise, without the body of Jesus, God's salvation plan would have never happened for us. Paul teaches this in his magnificent statement concerning Christ, in Philippians:

> Who, being in very nature God, did not consider equality with God something to be grasped, but made himself nothing, taking the very nature of a servant, *being made in human likeness*. And being found in appearance as a man, he humbled himself and became obedient to death—even death on a cross! (Philippians 2:6–8; emphasis added)

Overlaid with Gold

"Overlay the *frames with gold* and make gold rings to hold the crossbars. Also overlay the crossbars with gold" (Exodus 26:29; emphasis added).

Gold, the most valuable of all metals, is always a symbol of the deity and splendor of Christ. This is significant. The gold took the shape of the wood, in the same way as Christ's deity took the form of a human body. The God-man was needed to bring salvation. John tells us that the Word, referring to the humanity of Christ, was indeed God: "In the beginning was the Word, and *the Word was with God*, and the *Word was God*" (John 1:1; emphasis added).

Foundation of Silver Sockets

The sockets in which the frames rested were made of silver. In essence, the foundation of the tent was silver. This is different from the bronze sockets used in the outer fence frame: "Make twenty frames for the south side of the Tabernacle and make forty *silver* bases to go under them—two bases for each frame, one under each projection" (Exodus 26:18–19; emphasis added).

This use of silver is very important in the overall symbol of salvation, which the tabernacle depicted. The silver was obtained from the people as a result of a census and was called *atonement* or *ransom silver*. This precious metal was carried out from of the land of Egypt during the Exodus. In Israel, silver was collected in the form of a half shekel to buy certain protections and benefits for the people (emphasis added).

> When you take a *census* of the Israelites to count them, each one *must pay the* LORD *a ransom* for his life at the time he is counted. Then no plague will come on them when you number them. Each one who crosses over to those already counted is to give a half *shekel*, according to the sanctuary shekel, which weighs twenty gerahs. This half shekel is an offering to the LORD. (Exodus 30:12–13)

> The *silver* obtained from those of the community who were counted in the *census* was 100 talents and 1,775 shekels, according to the sanctuary shekel—one beka per person, that is, half a shekel, according to the sanctuary shekel, from everyone who had crossed over to those counted, twenty years old or more, a total of 603,550 men. The *100 talents of silver* were used to cast the bases for the sanctuary and for the curtain—100 bases from the 100 talents, one talent for each base. (Exodus 38:25–27)

Before the Israelites could experience the salvation of the Lord in the tabernacle, they had to participate in the redemption or ransom process based on silver. Redemption and salvation are closely linked. The concept of atonement money pictures the redeeming work of Christ in several ways.

We Were Redeemed (Bought) by Christ

Silver sockets held up the foundation of the tabernacle, and the payment of redemption money by the people provided the silver. Scripture clearly teaches that the foundation of our salvation is our redemption, a payment for our sins made by Jesus Christ (emphasis added).

> Keep watch over yourselves and all the flock of which the Holy Spirit has made you overseers. Be shepherds of the church of God, which he *bought with his own blood.* (Acts 20:28)

> He *redeemed* us in order that the blessing given to Abraham might come to the Gentiles through Christ Jesus, so that by faith we might receive the promise of the Spirit. (Galatians 3:14)

> You were *bought* at a price. Therefore honor God with your body. (1 Corinthians 6:20)

In the Old Testament tabernacle, by requiring silver to be a part of the construction process, God was showing the people that they could not participate in His salvation process if there was no redemption of silver. The New Testament reiterates that we cannot participate in salvation without being redeemed by Christ. In both cases, redemption is necessary.

Everyone Paid Redemption Money

We read in the book of Exodus that all who participated in God's plan had to pay redemption money: "When you take a census of the Israelites to count them, *each one must pay* the LORD a ransom for his life at the time he is counted. Then no plague will come on them when you number them" (Exodus 30:12; emphasis added).

Everyone participated in this redemption plan. No one could take part in the tabernacle process unless he had contributed redemption silver. In the New Testament, it is clear that all who participate in Christ's salvation must be redeemed. There is no other way to enter into salvation. He paid the price for everyone: "All the prophets testify about him that *everyone who believes* in him receives forgiveness of sins through his name" (Acts 10:43;

emphasis added) and "For Christ's love compels us, because we are convinced that *one died for all*, and therefore all died" (2 Corinthians 5:14; emphasis added).

All Gave the Same Amount

"The rich are not to give more than a *half shekel* and the poor are not to give less when you make the offering to the LORD *to atone for your lives*" (Exodus 30:15; emphasis added).

When it came to the redemption money, everyone contributed an equal share. The rich and poor both gave a half shekel. The atonement money was the same for everyone, regardless of status or financial means. Likewise for the New Testament believer, when it comes to our redemption in Christ, we all come in the same way regardless of our status. Everyone enters salvation on the basis of the same redemption requirement, the blood of Jesus. "Salvation is found in no one else, for there is *no other name* under heaven given to men by which we must be saved" (Acts 4:12; emphasis added).

No One Paid for Someone Else

Scripture reveals that each person was responsible for his or her own redemption money. No one could give money for someone else. "When you take a census of the Israelites to count them, *each one must pay* the LORD a *ransom* for his life at the time he is counted" (Exodus 30:12; emphasis added).

Every person stood on his or her own in this endeavor. This is symbolic of the fact that the New Testament is clear that we must come to the Lord individually. No one can come for us. Salvation is an individual decision. "Yet to all who received him, *to those who believed* in his name, he gave the right to become children of God" (John 1:12; emphasis added).

The Four Coverings

The tabernacle proper was basically a tent. The tent was layered with four different coverings designed to protect it from the elements and the extreme heat of the desert. Each layer in its own way was symbolic of Jesus. These coverings convey a rich meaning when it comes to aspects of our salvation in Christ.

The First (Inner) Covering was Made of Multicolored Linen

The first of the four coverings mentioned was made of white twisted linen and an assortment of colorful yarns. This layer was the most splendid in color of the four coverings. "All the skilled men among the workmen made the Tabernacle with ten curtains of *finely twisted linen* and *blue, purple* and *scarlet yarn*, with *cherubim* worked into them by a skilled craftsman" (Exodus 36:8; emphasis added).

It was also the inner covering of the tent. One had to be on the inside to behold this covering. What a picture of salvation! One cannot appreciate the beauty of Jesus and His work until he comes into a personal relationship with Him. In essence, we need an inside look. Paul contrasts the perceptional difference of spiritual dimensions between the one who knows Christ and the one who does not: "The man without the Spirit *does not accept the things that come from the Spirit of God*, for they are foolishness to him, and he cannot understand them, because they are spiritually discerned. The *spiritual man makes judgments about all things*, but he himself is not subject to any man's judgment" (1 Corinthians 2:14–15; emphasis added).

The attractiveness of Christ was not in His outward appearance, but was inside Him. The four colors in this covering were symbolic of Jesus. These colors also represent the four Gospels. These four themes of perfect humanity, deity, royalty, and death are consistently woven in throughout the tabernacle.

- Purple: Signified the royalty of Jesus (Gospel of Matthew)
- Red: Symbolized the blood of Jesus (Gospel of Mark)

- White: Symbolized Jesus's perfect humanity (Gospel of Luke)
- Blue: Signified that He was the Son of God (Gospel of John)

Also, we are introduced for the first time to cherubim, which were included in the design of this inner covering. They are a symbol of the justice and holy righteousness of the Lord. We will meet these high-level spirit beings later in other places of the tabernacle, where we will discuss their significance in great detail.

The Second Covering was Made of Goat Hair

"They made curtains of *goat hair* for the tent over the Tabernacle—eleven all together" (Exodus 36:14; emphasis added).

In the Old Testament, goats were sin bearers.

> He shall sprinkle some of the blood on it with his finger seven times to cleanse it and to consecrate it from the uncleanness of the Israelites. When Aaron has finished making atonement for the Most Holy Place, the Tent of Meeting and the altar, he shall bring forward the live *goat*. He is to lay both hands on the head of the live *goat* and *confess over it all the wickedness and rebellion of the Israelites—all their sins*—and put them on the goat's head. He shall send the goat away into the desert in the care of a man appointed for the task. The *goat will carry on itself all their sins* to a solitary place; and the man shall release it in the desert. (Leviticus 16:19–22; emphasis added)

We will explain the significance of the goat when we later discuss the Day of Atonement, but it is obvious that the goat was the one animal that represented the bearing and taking away of sins. This is a picture of Jesus: the one who would ultimately bear the sins of the whole world. "He himself *bore our sins* in his body on the tree, so that we might die to sins and live for righteousness; by his wounds you have been healed. (1 Peter 2:24; emphasis added).

The Third Covering was Made of Ram Skin

"Then they made for the tent a covering of *ram skins dyed red*" (Exodus 36:19; emphasis added).

The ram was the symbol for a substitute. This is poignantly illustrated in the story of Abraham and Isaac. "Abraham looked up and there in a thicket he saw a *ram* caught by its horns. He went over and took the ram and sacrificed it as a burnt offering instead of his son" (Genesis 22:13; emphasis added).

The ram was used as a substitute for Isaac on the altar of Abraham. This sacrifice symbolized that one day, Christ would take our place on the cross and become our substitute. The red color highlights the blood of Christ which would be shed for us: "The next day John saw Jesus coming toward him and said, 'Look, the *Lamb of God*, who takes away the sin of the world!'" (John 1:29; emphasis added).

The Fourth (Outer) Covering was Made of Sea Cow Skin

"Then they made for the tent...a covering of *hides of sea cows*" (Exodus 36:19; emphasis added).

Some translations (KJV) render the Hebrew word as *badger skin*. However, most modern scholars believe this skin was from a maritime animal such as a porpoise or dugong probably brought out of Egypt during the Exodus. It was a tough leather utilized by Israel to make shoes (Ezekiel 16:10). This sea cow skin was the one visible from the outside. It was also the most unattractive.

A Picture of Christ

Here we have an important picture of Jesus Christ. Just as the outer skin hid the beauty and splendor of the other coverings, Christ's body concealed all the beauty and splendor of deity that was inside of Him. The magnificence of heaven was wrapped in an ordinary, unassuming package. This was a focus of the Old Testament prophet Isaiah: "He grew up before him like a tender shoot, and like a root out of dry ground. He had *no beauty or majesty to attract us to him*, nothing in his appearance that we should desire him" (Isaiah 53:2; emphasis added).

In this verse, Isaiah is describing the suffering servant-Messiah, who was to come. This does not mean that Jesus was hideous or repulsive to behold, but it does underscore the point that He was not spectacular in His appearance. The New Testament echoes a similar theme in Philippians: "But made *himself nothing*, taking the very nature of a servant, being made in human likeness. And being found in appearance as a man, he humbled himself and became obedient to death—even death on a cross!" (Philippians 2:7–8; emphasis added).

When people beheld Jesus, they saw a human being just like themselves. They didn't realize that Christ's ordinary body was masking the splendor of God. When observers saw the plain sea cow skin on the outside of the tent, they would never have guessed that there was great beauty and glory inside.

A Picture of the Church

This image of the unspectacular outer covering of the tabernacle applies to the church as well. The attractiveness of the church in the world is not what can be seen from the outside, but from what emanates from the inside. The Apostle Paul captures this idea by comparing us to ordinary and unattractive earthly jars of clay, which contain the treasure and splendor of God's glory and light: "For God, who said, 'Let light shine out of darkness,' made his light shine in our hearts to give us the light of the knowledge of the glory of God in the face of Christ. But we have this *treasure in jars of clay* to show that this all-surpassing power is from God and not from us" (2 Corinthians 4:6–7; emphasis added).

When the church attempts to impress the world with money, massive programs, entertainment, power, garish buildings, or fame, she misses the point. What the world needs to see is the glorious work of Christ inside of us. This is what attracted people to Jesus, and the same is true of His followers. The marvel and wonder of the church is that God can do so many beautiful things through a very ordinary and unspectacular group of people.

The Ropes and Tent Pegs

The last items to be discussed in the general setup of the tabernacle proper are the ropes and pegs, which stabilized the tent. They picture two important aspects of salvation.

The Pegs Speak of Judgment

The tent pegs were made of bronze. Under our discussion of the bronze altar, we noted that bronze was the symbol of judgment, and it could withstand intense fire: "All the other articles used in the service of the Tabernacle, whatever their function, including all the *tent pegs* for it and those for the courtyard, are to be of *bronze*" (Exodus 27:19; emphasis added).

Tent pegs were essential to the stability of the tent. For our salvation to be stable, sin has to be judged by God. Without judgment, there can be no salvation. Since the tent pegs are placed in the ground and yet appear above the ground as well, some also see a picture of death and resurrection in them.

The Ropes Represent Love

Attached to the tent pegs were ropes, which kept the tent upright so that it could not be blown away: "The tent pegs for the Tabernacle and for the courtyard, and their *ropes*" (Exodus 35:18; emphasis added).

The Old Testament symbolically associates ropes with the love of God: "I led them with cords of human kindness, with *ties [ropes] of love*; I lifted the yoke from their neck and bent down to feed them" (Hosea 11:4)

The ropes used to stabilize the tabernacle may also represent the love of God. Love is attached to the pegs of judgment. There is a correlation here. It was the love of God that sent Jesus to pay for our judgment. Proper judgment is the foundation of salvation, but so is love. This point is reinforced in the New Testament: "But God demonstrates his own *love* for us in this: while we were still sinners, *Christ died* for us" (Romans 5:8; emphasis added).

The ropes and pegs gave the tent stability against the wind and other forces of nature. God's love makes our salvation secure and allows us to withstand the attacks of Satan.

A Tent With Two Divisions

The tabernacle proper was divided into two compartments, the holy place and the holy of holies (or the most holy place).

> Hang the curtain from the clasps and place the ark of the Testimony behind the curtain. The curtain will separate the *Holy Place* from the *Most Holy Place*. (Exodus 26:33)

> A Tabernacle was set up. In its first room were the lampstand, the table and the consecrated bread; this was called *the Holy Place*. Behind the second curtain was a room called *the Most Holy Place*. Hebrews 9:2–3 (emphasis added)

The holy place contained three primary pieces of furniture: the golden lampstand, the table of bread, and the altar of incense. The holy of holies (or most holy place) was where the Ark of the Covenant, the mercy seat, and the glory of the Lord resided. A veil separated these two compartments. The relationship between these two rooms is important. Before one can actually experience the intimacy, holy presence, and worship of God in the holy of holies, he must learn to connect to the Lord in the holy place. This is where prayer, acceptance, feeding on the bread of life, fellowshipping with God and fellow priests, and living under the anointing of the Spirit are emphasized. These are the practices of the priesthood that lead us into God's presence (the holy of holies). We will discuss and unwrap all of these items in detail in the next few chapters.

Gold-Gilded Boards on Silver Sockets

Curtains and Coverings of the Holy Place

DISCUSSION QUESTIONS

1. The bases holding the support poles were made of silver. In what way did this silver symbolize the salvation, which was to come in Christ?

2. How is the fact that everyone gave the same amount of atonement money a picture of our salvation?

3. Why was the outer skin on the outside of the tabernacle the least attractive covering? What does this tell us about Christ and our work on the earth?

4. Discuss the important relationship between the positioning of the holy place and holy of holies? How does this connection apply to the Christian experience today?

V

THE HOLY PLACE

6

The Golden Candlestick

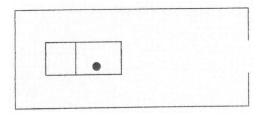

In the last chapter, we saw that the tabernacle proper was divided into the holy place and the holy of holies. The holy place was the center of the priestly spiritual activity in the tabernacle. It was where the priests spent most of their time in service to the Lord. The holy place contained three pieces of furniture: the golden candlestick, the table of bread, and the altar of incense. The golden candlestick, also referred to as a lampstand, was located on the south side of the holy place. "Place the table outside the curtain on the north side of the Tabernacle and put the *lampstand opposite it on the south side*" (Exodus 26:35; emphasis added).

This marvelous candelabra presented a wonderful picture of the relationship between Christ and His church. Here are a number of important symbolic aspects of the golden candlestick.

The Only Source of Light in the Holy Place

The candles on the golden candlestick provided the only light in the holy place. The courtyard was illumined with natural sunlight, while the holy of holies radiated the light of the glory of God. The candlestick pictures Christ as the only light of the world:

"While I am in the world, *I am* the light of the world" John 9:5; emphasis added).

As we noticed under our discussion of the gate, Jesus used the intensive form in the Greek, *ego eimi,* for the phrase "I am." Accurately translated, this phrase means, *I, and no one else, am the light.* John the Baptist was the first person to introduce this Light to the world. "He came as a witness to testify concerning *that light,* so that through him all men might believe" (John 1:7; emphasis added).

It is important also to note that in the same way the candlestick was the only light in the holy place, the church is the only light of Jesus in the world. We are His beautiful light, and it is important that we shine. Jesus said this about us:

> *You are the light* of the world. A city on a hill cannot be hidden. Neither do people light a lamp and put it under a bowl. Instead they put it on its stand, and it gives light to everyone in the house. In the same way, *let your light shine* before men, that they may see your good deeds and praise your Father in heaven. (Matthew 5:14–16; emphasis added)

The Apostle Paul reiterates the words of Jesus in the book of Ephesians: "For you were once darkness, but now *you are light* in the Lord. Live as children of *light* (for the fruit of the light consists in all goodness, righteousness and truth)" (Ephesians 5:8–9; emphasis added).

Our lifestyle before the watching world is indispensable for our light to shine. People will not listen to what we have to say if our deportment is not reflecting the light of the Lord Jesus Christ. It is often the false Jesus of dead religion and legalism, projected by misguided Christians, the world rejects. Our mission is to present to those outside of Christ the light of the biblical Jesus, not a poor imitation which only leads to darkness.

Pure, Hammered Gold Construction

The golden candlestick was made of pure gold, whereas the other pieces of furniture were merely overlaid with gold. The lampstand was also forged by a blacksmith, who repeatedly struck and hammered the gold to shape it. "Make a lampstand of *pure gold* and *hammer* it out, base and shaft" (Exodus 25:31; emphasis added).

This is a dual picture of the Lord Jesus Christ. Gold symbolizes His worth, deity, and splendor. He is the Son of God sent from heaven's glory. However, the fact that the gold had to be hammered foreshadows the brutal treatment received by the Lord Jesus Christ to provide the foundation for this light. Notice the vivid description Isaiah employs to describe our Lord's violent death: "But he was *pierced* for our transgressions, he was *crushed* for our iniquities; the *punishment* that brought us peace was upon him, and by his *wounds* we are healed. We all, like sheep, have gone astray, each of us has turned to his own way; and the LORD has laid on him the iniquity of us all" (Isaiah 53:5–6; emphasis added).

God predicted through the prophet that Jesus, the Messiah, would suffer a terrible and horrible death. The New Testament records the fulfillment of this prophecy (emphasis added): "Did not the Christ have to *suffer* these things and then enter his glory? (Luke 24:26) and "In bringing many sons to glory, it was fitting that God, for whom and through whom everything exists, should make the author of their salvation perfect through *suffering*" (Hebrews 2:10).

A Shaft with Foliage on It

The golden candlestick was adorned with flowers, buds, and blossoms. "Its *flowerlike* cups, *buds* and *blossoms* shall be of one piece with it" (Exodus 25:31; emphasis added).

The image of flowers and blossoms elicits pictures of growth and life. In essence, this light of the candlestick would be associated with life in the form of vegetation and flowers. These vibrant images of nature are often associated with Jesus and the Christian life. The church is a light, which also produces fruit. Jesus used the analogy of the vine and branches to illustrate the fruit bearing process between His followers and Himself (emphasis added):

> I am the *true vine*, and my Father is the gardener. (John 15:1)

> Remain in me, and I will remain in you. No branch can *bear fruit* by itself; it must remain in the vine. Neither can you *bear fruit* unless you remain in me. I am the vine; *you are the branches*. If a man remains in me and I in him, he will *bear much fruit*; apart from me you can do nothing. (John 15:4–5)

The Bible also speaks of the believer's life, producing the fruit of the Spirit. This fruit is literally the life of Christ emanating from the believer. As we shall see later, the candlestick was fueled by oil representing the Holy Spirit: "But the *fruit of the Spirit* is love, joy, peace, patience, kindness, goodness, faithfulness" (Galatians 5:22; emphasis added).

Six Branches from the Sides

Every aspect of the tabernacle encapsulates some symbolic meaning regarding salvation. No detail was wasted. The symbolism in the branches of the candlestick speaks of the church and her relationship to Jesus, the light. "*Six branches are to extend from the sides* of the lampstand—three on one side and three on the other" (Exodus 25:32; emphasis added).

Six is the Number of Man; He is Completed When Joined to Jesus

Man was created on the sixth day. However, he was not complete until he was able to step into the seventh day, which was God's Sabbath day. In other words, man's first full day after his creation was on God's Sabbath day of rest. This is profoundly important as it illustrates the human race can only find meaning when he is in relationship with the Creator. Similarly, in regard to salvation, man is only spiritually complete when joined to Jesus. Our ability to be light sources is dependent on our connection to Him. Christ Himself refers to this fact: "I am the vine; you are the branches. *If a man remains in me* and I in him, he will bear much fruit; apart from me you can do nothing" (John 15:5).

The Branches Came Out of the Side, and We Came Out of Jesus's Side

The significance of the side is important. Jesus was not officially declared dead until His side was pierced. This was the final indication that the Son of God had indeed expired on the cross. In essence, the church ultimately came out of Jesus's death (emphasis added): "But he was *pierced* for our transgressions" (Isaiah 53:5) and "Instead, one of the soldiers pierced *Jesus' side* with a spear, bringing a sudden flow of blood and water" (John 19:34).

The Branches Held up the Main Light

Standing in the midst of the six branches was the main light of the lampstand. The branches held up the dominate candle. What a picture of the church! We hold the light of Jesus up to the world. The New Testament affirms this point: "*You are the light* of the world. A city on a hill cannot be hidden" (Matthew 5:14; emphasis added).

In this passage, Jesus is affirming to the disciples that they will bear His light to the world. In the book of Revelation, we are given a depiction of Jesus, standing in the midst of the lampstands or candlesticks. The Light of the world is positioned in the middle of His light-bearing churches, encouraging them to stay true to the faith. This is a clear picture and fulfillment of the candlestick in the tabernacle: "I turned around to see the voice that was speaking to me. And when I turned I saw seven golden *lampstands*, and among the *lampstands* was someone like a son of man" (Revelation 1:12–13; emphasis added).

The Lamps Always Burning

The lamps burned continually in the holy place. This perpetual light was the constant reminder Jesus's light would always shine on the earth. "In the Tent of Meeting, outside the curtain that is in front of the Testimony, Aaron and his sons are to *keep the lamps burning* before the LORD from evening till morning. This is to be a lasting ordinance among the Israelites for the generations to come" (Exodus 27:21; emphasis added).

The branches would never cease to carry His light to the world. Evil forces for centuries have attempted to extinguish the light of Christ through persecution and oppression, but no matter how great the darkness may seem in our time, the light of Christ will never stop shining. This is the hope for the world. Satan will try and extinguish the light, but he will fail (emphasis added): "In him was life, and that life was the *light of men*. The light *shines in the darkness*, but the darkness has not understood it" (John 1:4–5) and "He himself was not the light; he came only as a witness to the light. The *true light* that gives light to every man was coming into the world" (John 1:8–9).

Pure Oil in the Lamps

The light was required to be fueled by pure, clear oil. "Command the Israelites to bring you *clear oil of pressed olives* for the light so that the lamps may be kept burning" (Exodus 27:20; emphasis added).

In the Bible, oil is symbolic of the anointing of the Holy Spirit. The prophets Isaiah and Zechariah unequivocally associated the olive oil with the anointing of the Holy Spirit (emphasis added):

> The *Spirit* of the Sovereign LORD is on me, because the LORD has *anointed* me to preach good news to the poor. (Isaiah 61:1)

> He asked me, "What do you see?" I answered, "I see a solid gold lampstand with a bowl at the top and seven lights on it, with seven channels to the lights. Also there are *two olive*

trees by it, one on the right of the bowl and the other on its left." I asked the angel who talked with me, "What are these, my lord?" So he said to me, "This is the word of the LORD to Zerubbabel: 'Not by might nor by power, but by my *Spirit* says the LORD Almighty.'" (Zechariah 4:2–4, 6)

The light of Jesus will shine through those who are empowered by the Holy Spirit. This is what Jesus meant when He spoke prior to His ascension: "But you will receive *power* when the *Holy Spirit* comes on you; and you will be my *witnesses* in Jerusalem, and in all Judea and Samaria, and to the ends of the earth" (Acts 1:8; emphasis added).

Trimmed Wicks

The wicks were required to be trimmed and kept clean. Dirty wicks would diminish and impede the light: "They are to take a blue cloth and cover the lampstand that is for light, together with its lamps, its *wick trimmers* and trays, and all its jars for the oil used to supply it" (Numbers 4:9; emphasis added).

This fact symbolizes the believer's need to stay clean as well. When our lives are full of sin and disobedience, the work of the Holy Spirit is hindered, and the light of Christ diminishes. The New Testament supports this point (emphasis added): "For you *were once darkness, but now you are light* in the Lord. *Live as children of light* (for the fruit of the light consists in all goodness, righteousness and truth) and find out what pleases the Lord" (Ephesians 5:8–10) and "Everyone who has this hope in him *purifies himself*, just as he is pure (1 John 3:3).

The Golden Candlestick

DISCUSSION QUESTIONS

1. Why was the candlestick the only light in the holy place? What did this symbolize?
2. What is the significance of the six branches coming out of the side of the candlestick?
3. What aspect of the candlestick does Acts 1:8 represent?
4. How does God shine His light on the earth today? What can stop the light from shining?
5. Using the instruction on the golden candlestick, what hope would you give to those whose only focus is on how dark our world is?

7

The Table of Bread

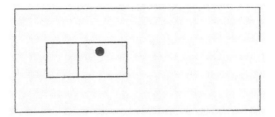

The second major piece of furniture in the holy place was the table of bread located on the north side. "Place the *table [bread]* outside the curtain on the *north side* of the Tabernacle and put the lampstand opposite it on the south side" (Exodus 26:35; emphasis added).

The table of bread was the smallest piece of furniture in the holy place, and it was where fellowship and camaraderie among the priests took place. There are many interesting symbolic aspects of Christ and salvation in this table.

Acacia Wood and Gold Construction

Like some other pieces of furniture in the tabernacle, the table of bread was made of acacia wood and overlaid with gold: "Make a table of *acacia wood*—two cubits long, a cubit wide and a cubit and a half high. Overlay it with pure gold and make a gold molding around it" (Exodus 25:23–24; emphasis added).

Again, this is a picture of Christ. The wood represents His humanity, and the gold represents His deity. These two come together as they did in Christ. Deity took the shape of humanity.

A Place of Fellowship Among the Priests

The table of bread was a place of fellowship for the priests, and it was the only area in the tabernacle where they could eat. They spent time with each other in the presence of the Lord. "This bread is to be set out before the LORD regularly, Sabbath after Sabbath, on behalf of the Israelites, as a lasting covenant. It belongs to *Aaron and his sons, who are to eat it in a holy place*, because it is a most holy part of their regular share of the offerings made to the LORD by fire" (Leviticus 24:8–9; emphasis added).

This is a wonderful picture of what New Testament priests do as well. The Bible speaks of our fellowship with the Father and our fellowship with each other (fellow priests): "We proclaim to you what we have seen and heard, so that you also may have *fellowship with us.* And our fellowship is with the Father and with his Son, Jesus Christ" (1 John 1:3; emphasis added).

Fellowship is not relationship. Fellowship describes the interaction and friendship among those with whom we share something in common. In the Old Testament, the priests shared a common function of serving Jehovah God and His people through the tabernacle ministry. In the New Testament, the priesthood of the church shares a fellowship based on our relationship to Christ and our mandated mission of taking this wonderful gospel of the risen Savior to the world.

This table of bread also foreshadowed the day when the New Testament priests would enjoy fellowship around the Lord's table, celebrating their Savior. The communion (or Eucharist) we participate in today has its roots in the tabernacle. When we participate in communion, we are celebrating together our relationship with Christ. "Is not the cup of thanksgiving for which we give thanks a *participation* in the blood of Christ? And is not the bread that we break a *participation* in the body of Christ? *Because there is one loaf, we, who are many, are one body*, for we all partake of the one loaf" (1 Corinthians 10:16–17).

A Table of Bread

The main focus of the table was the bread placed upon it. The bread is richly symbolic of Jesus Christ. Every detail was significant.

The Bread Signified Jesus, the Bread of Life

The bread on the table ultimately foreshadowed Jesus Christ, who is the bread of life. The manna in the wilderness also was a shadow of Christ (Exodus 16). The bread emphasized the fact that the only spiritual food humanity needs is based on Him. He is the bread of life (emphasis added): "Then Jesus declared, '*I am the bread of life.* He who comes to me will never go hungry, and he who believes in me will never be thirsty'" (John 6:35) and "Jesus said to them, 'I tell you the truth, unless you *eat the flesh* of the Son of Man and drink his blood, you have no life in you'" (John 6:53).

Jesus, while having supper with His disciples, declared that the bread represented His body, which was to eventually be sacrificed: "And he took bread, gave thanks and broke it, and gave it to them, saying, "*This is my body* given for you; do this in remembrance of me" (Luke 22:19; emphasis added).

Jesus, the bread of life, would give His life that we might receive spiritual nourishment. Salvation is a process of continually feeding on and partaking of Jesus, the bread of life. When we partake of the bread during communion, it is not only to celebrate what Christ did in the past but also to participate in what He can do for us every day.

The Twelve Loaves Represented Israel and Now Represent the Church

Twelve loaves of bread were set out in two rows of six on the table: "Take fine flour and bake twelve loaves of bread, using two-tenths of an ephah for each loaf. Set them in *two rows, six in each row*, on the table of pure gold before the LORD" (Leviticus 24:5–6; emphasis added).

The number twelve is representative of the twelve tribes of Israel, the Old Testament people of God. In fact, we are told specifically that it was on behalf of the Israelites. "This bread is to be set out before the LORD regularly, Sabbath after Sabbath, on *behalf of the Israelites*, as a lasting covenant" (Leviticus 24:8).

The loaves symbolized that ultimately Christ is the only one who can establish a people relationally with God. In the New Testament, there are two bodies of Christ: His physical, ascended body, and His universal church body. The communion bread not only depicts Christ's physical body but also His church body. Paul affirms this (emphasis added): "And God placed all things under his feet and appointed him to be head over everything for the *church, which is his body*, the fullness of him who fills everything in every way" (Ephesians 1:22–23) and "Because there is *one loaf, we, who are many, are one body*, for we all partake of the one loaf" (1 Corinthians 10:17).

The physical body of Christ is related to a spiritual body. Just as the bread on the table represented the people of God in the Old Testament, the bread on the communion table stands for us, the people of God in the New Testament (His church).

The Bread Illustrated Mankind's Acceptance into the Presence of God

The bread on the table was also called the *bread of the presence*. This sacred term was used because the bread was set before Jehovah's presence with His face gazing upon it (emphasis added): "Put the *bread of the Presence* on this table to be before me at all times" (Exodus 25:30) and "Over the *table of the Presence* they are to spread a blue cloth and put on it the plates, dishes and bowls, and the jars for drink offerings; the bread that is continually there is to remain on it" (Numbers 4:7).

God was not ashamed to look down upon these loaves, which represented His relationship with Israel. The bread also ultimately symbolized the relationship we have with God because of Jesus.

We have acceptance in God's presence. Scripture beautifully states this point: "Therefore, since we have been justified through faith, we have *peace with God* through our Lord Jesus Christ" (Romans 5:1; emphasis added).

The Greek word translated for "with" is *pros*, and it means *face-to-face*. Literally, this verse teaches us that we have peace in the face of God. This is a positional peace, not an emotional peace. The believer doesn't have to be ashamed to come into the presence of God. He has peace in the face of God by the blood of Jesus Christ. The New Testament also affirms that we have fellowship with God by the blood of the Lamb: "We proclaim to you what we have seen and heard, so that you also may have fellowship with us. And our *fellowship is with the Father* and with his Son, Jesus Christ" (1 John 1:3).

The Bread was the Only Source of Food in the Holy Place

There was no other food in the holy place besides the bread. This fact underscores the point that Christ is the only source of spiritual nourishment that we need to live productively in God. We must feed off the living Jesus to live a fulfilled Christian life: "Then Jesus declared, '*I am* the bread of life. He who comes to me will never go hungry'" (John 6:35; emphasis added).

As we have noted in other places, the translation "I am" is from the Greek phrase, *ego eimi*, and is an intensive way of saying, *I and only I am the true bread from heaven*.

The bread also symbolizes the Word of God in any form it is given (spoken or written). When offered physical bread during His wilderness experience, Jesus spoke of the importance of living on God's Word: "Jesus answered, 'It is written: "Man does not live on bread alone, but on every *word that comes from the mouth of God*"' (Matthew 4:4; emphasis added).

Paul speaks of the importance of God's Word in our lives for growth and warfare (emphasis added): "*All Scripture is God-breathed and is useful* for teaching, rebuking, correcting and training in righteousness, so that the man of God may be thoroughly equipped for every good work" (2 Timothy 3:16–17) and "Take the helmet of salvation and the sword of the Spirit, which is the *word of God*" (Ephesians 6:17).

Fresh Bread was To Be Present at All Times

"Put the bread of the Presence on this table to be *before me at all times*" (Exodus 25:30) and "This bread is to be set out before the Lord *regularly, Sabbath after Sabbath*, on behalf of the Israelites, as a lasting covenant" (Leviticus 24:8). (emphasis added)

The bread was to be continuously present before the Lord at the table. This emphasized God's covenant relationship with Israel. His people were always before Him. This symbolically pictured that Christ, the living bread, would continue to live on and always be present for His people as the bread of life. The bread was kept fresh to depict the fact that Jesus, the bread of life, would never become stale or old. In the Old Testament, when Israel gathered the manna (another symbol of Christ), they had to gather it fresh every day. The only exception was on the day before the Sabbath, when they could gather twice the daily amount:

> Then the Lord said to Moses, "I will rain down bread from heaven for you. The people are to *go out each day and gather enough for that day*. In this way I will test them and see whether they will follow my instructions. On the sixth day they are to prepare what they bring in, and that is to be twice as much as they gather on the other days. (Exodus 16:4–5; emphasis added).

God wanted them to enjoy fresh blessings from His hand. We must feed off Jesus daily. He is fresh every day. Jesus will never become an old, stale, crusty piece of bread to us. He will feed us with fresh bread that leads to life on a daily basis. That is why Jesus exhorted His disciples to feed on Him: "Just as the living Father sent me and I live because of the Father, *so the one who feeds on me will live because of me*. This is the *bread* that came down from heaven. Your forefathers ate manna and died, but he who feeds on this bread will live forever" (John 6:57–58; emphasis added).

Incense Alongside the Bread

"Along each row put some pure *incense* as a memorial portion to represent the bread and to be an offering made to the LORD by fire" (Leviticus 24:7; emphasis added).

In scripture, incense represents the acceptance of a sweet-smelling sacrifice. Here, the incense speaks of Christ, the bread of life and His sacrifice for our sins being accepted by God. Because His sacrifice was acceptable before the Lord, salvation became complete, and Jesus would continue on as the living bread of life. This incense reminds us that Jesus's sacrifice was acceptable to God, and thus, as His followers, we are acceptable to God. God is pleased with us (emphasis added):

> Live a life filled with love for others, following the example of Christ, who loved you and gave himself as a sacrifice to take away your sins. And *God was pleased, because that sacrifice was like sweet perfume to him.* (Ephesians 5:2)

> The blood of goats and bulls and the ashes of a heifer sprinkled on those who are ceremonially unclean sanctify them so that they are outwardly clean. How much more, then, will the blood of Christ, who through the eternal Spirit offered himself unblemished to God, *cleanse our consciences from acts that lead to death*, so that we may serve the living God! (Hebrews 9:13–14)

No Chairs at the Table

Oddly, scripture never mentions the presence of chairs at the table of bread or anywhere else in the tabernacle. This is somewhat strange. Normally, one would expect to find chairs around a table of fellowship. The reason that no chairs are mentioned is that the priests were not allowed to sit down. The Old Testament priests were not perfect. Their work was never done. They could not rest because they were always having to deal with sin: their own and those of the people. Sitting would represent finality. Only one priest in the entire Bible was allowed to sit down, and that was Jesus Christ. He finished the work. The symbolism in the tabernacle was one of imperfection, and there was never a sense of total rest. Jesus perfected the work of salvation. Therefore, He could sit down. The New Testament expounds on this.

The Cross Speaks of Finality

In John 19:30, while hanging on the cross, Jesus uttered these famous words, "When he had received the drink, Jesus said, *'It is finished.'* With that, he bowed his head and gave up his spirit. (emphasis added)

The Greek word translated "it is finished" is a perfect tense form of the word, *teleō*, which can mean the *end* or *completion*. The Greek perfect tense often conveys the idea of a completed action with results that continue. In this verse, when Jesus stated, "It is finished," He was declaring the work of salvation was finished on the cross with the result that it is still finished. This high priest finished the work, and no one will need to come along and do anything else to secure and procure our salvation.

Jesus Sat Down

We have discussed that there were no provisions for the priests to sit down in the tabernacle, illustrating that their work was never done. However, when Jesus completed the work of salvation, the Bible declares He sat down. This was an action of finality.

> The Son is the radiance of God's glory and the exact representation of his being, sustaining all things by his powerful word. After he had provided purification for sins, *he sat down* at the right hand of the Majesty in heaven. (Hebrews 1:3)

> But when this priest had offered for all time one sacrifice for sins, he *sat down* at the right hand of God. (Hebrews 10:12)

> Let us fix our eyes on Jesus, the author and perfecter of our faith, who for the joy set before him endured the cross, scorning its shame, and *sat down* at the right hand of the throne of God. (Hebrews 12:2) (emphasis added)

Jesus could sit down because there was nothing left to do. Salvation starts for us from a point of completion.

There was One Exception

Presently, the Lord is seated at the right hand of the Father. But Jesus will make an exception to stand while welcoming His martyrs. Only one place is it recorded in scripture that Jesus stood up, and that was at the stoning of Stephen the martyr: "But Stephen, full of the Holy Spirit, looked up to heaven and saw the glory of God, and Jesus standing at the right hand of God. 'Look,' he said, 'I see heaven open and the *Son of Man standing* at the right hand of God.'" (Acts 7:55–56; emphasis added).

He sits because He has finished the work of salvation. There is nothing left to do because Jesus has completed the job. Salvation begins from a place of rest. Too many believers are working very hard to achieve acceptance before God. Our most productive work can only come when we start from the rest Jesus provides at the throne of God.

A Gold Rim Around the Table

"Also make around it a rim a handbreadth wide and put a *gold molding on the rim*" (Exodus 25:25; emphasis added).

The rim was designed to protect the bread from falling off the table and becoming defiled, symbolizing the fact salvation in Christ is secure. Christ protects us, and we are safe in Him. Jesus Himself said, "I give them eternal life, and *they shall never perish*; no one can snatch them out of my hand" (John 10:28).

The bread, depicting Israel, was safe and secure on the table. It is comforting and reassuring to know that we are safe and secure in Christ.

Transported on Poles by Priests

Like the bronze altar, the table of bread was to be transported by priests. "The rings are to be close to the rim to hold the poles used in *carrying the table*" (Exodus 25:27; emphasis added).

Priests carried the table through the desert on poles. This symbolizes the fact that wherever we go, the bread of life sustains us, even in the midst of difficulty and hardship. David put it this way: "*You prepare a table* before me in the presence of my enemies. You anoint my head with oil; my cup overflows" (Psalm 23:5; emphasis added).

The bread of life feeds and sustains us in every situation. The carrying of the table of bread also typifies the church, transporting the bread of life to the world. We, the priesthood of Christ, carry the living bread and offer this spiritual nourishment to every person on earth.

The Table of Shewbread

DISCUSSION QUESTIONS

1. There were twelve loaves on the table of bread? Of what was this symbolic, and how does this apply to the New Testament church?

2. The bread was identified with the presence of God. What was the significance of this "presence," and how does this relate to us today?

3. What is the symbolic significance that the bread was the only source of food in the holy place? What does this mean for the Christian life?

4. Why were there no chairs provided at the table? What did this picture? How did this change in the New Testament and why?

5. Knowing what we do about the table of bread. How should this impact the way we take and receive communion today?

8

The Altar of Incense

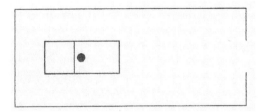

The golden candlestick depicted the priests, carrying forth the light and fruit of Jesus to the world as they are anointed by the Holy Spirit. The table of bread symbolized the daily fellowship the priests experienced with God and one another, through Jesus, the bread of life. The third piece of furniture in the holy place, the altar of incense, represented the believer's acceptance before the throne of God and access to Him through prayer and worship, now made possible by Christ. It was located in the holy place in front of the veil. This piece of furniture was closer to the holy of holies than either the golden candlestick or the table of bread.

> Make an *altar of acacia wood for burning incense*. It is to be square, a cubit long and a cubit wide, and two cubits high—its horns of one piece with it. Overlay the top and all the sides and the horns with pure gold, and make a gold molding around it. Make two gold rings for the altar below the molding—two on opposite sides—to hold the poles used to carry it. Make the poles of acacia wood and overlay them with gold. *Put the altar in front of the curtain* that is before the ark of the Testimony—before the atonement cover that

is over the Testimony—where I will meet with you. (Exodus 30:1–6; emphasis added).

The altar of incense symbolizes in a striking way that we can come boldly to the throne of God because of what Christ has accomplished on the cross.

Acacia Wood and Gold Construction

Like other items in the tabernacle, the altar of incense was constructed of acacia wood and covered with gold. As we have noted before, this represents the body and deity of Christ. Similar to the table of bread, this altar displays that the way to God comes through the God-man, Jesus Christ, who lives eternally in the heavens to represent us before God. An understanding of our acceptance and access to God is essential to living a productive and fruitful Christian life. The altar of incense speaks volumes in this regard.

A Picture of Our Acceptance Before the Throne of God

Whereas the bronze altar of sacrifice was an altar of judgment, the altar of incense is a marvelous representation of our *acceptance* by God through the Lord Jesus Christ, which allows us access to His throne. The reason we can freely pray to the Lord is that we now have a pathway to God because of what Christ has accomplished. There are many facets to this acceptance.

We Have Acceptance Because Through Christ All of Our Past Sins are Forgiven

Jesus has gone before the throne of God to intercede on our behalf. Therefore, we have a position of forgiveness before God. All past sins are erased: "For Christ did not enter a man-made sanctuary that was only a copy of the true one; he entered heaven itself, now *to appear for us in God's presence*" (Hebrews 9:24) and "Therefore he is able to *save completely* those who come to God through him, because he *always lives to intercede for them*" (Hebrews 7:25). (emphasis added)

We Have Acceptance Because Through Christ Daily Sins are Forgiven

Jesus is depicted in the New Testament as an advocate (lawyer) or intercessor on behalf of the saints for sins committed after we are born again. When we sin, we can confess that sin, knowing that Jesus is interceding with His blood to ask forgiveness: "My dear children, I write this to you so that you will not sin. But *if anybody does sin*, we have *one who speaks* to the Father in our *defense—Jesus Christ*, the Righteous One" (1 John 2:1; emphasis added).

We Have Acceptance Because Through Christ Our Accusers have Been Silenced

The Bible defines Satan as an accuser of the saints. In fact, another common name of our adversary, devil, means *accuser*. He indicts God of being unfair in allowing us to have a relationship with Him. He charges us of unworthiness to be in God's family. Jesus has nullified these accusations by His blood:

> *Who is he that condemns?* Christ Jesus, who died—more than that, who was raised to life—is at the right hand of God and is also interceding for us. (Romans 8:34)

> Then I heard a loud voice in heaven say: "Now have come the salvation and the power and the kingdom of our God, and the authority of his Christ. For the *accuser of our brothers*, who accuses them before our God day and night, has been hurled down." (Revelation 12:10) (emphasis added)

As our defense lawyer, Christ is continually representing us before God. His blood and prayers on our behalf keep us secure in the Father's presence. The altar of incense symbolizes the intercession of Jesus on our behalf.

A Symbol of Our Intercession in Prayer and Worship

The altar of incense not only represents the believers' acceptance before God but also underscores our *access* in prayer and worship before the throne. Because of the blood shed on the altar of sacrifice, the believer can now freely enter into God's presence at the altar of incense. In many ways, this altar symbolizes the believer's power before the throne of God.

Incense Symbolizes Prayer

In the Bible, incense is a picture of prayer and worship. Our prayers have a sweet-smelling fragrance that literally wafts upward to the very nostrils of God:

> May my *prayer be set before you like incense*; may the lifting up of my hands be like the evening sacrifice. (Psalm 141:2)

> And when he had taken it, the four living creatures and the twenty-four elders fell down before the Lamb. Each one had a harp and they were holding golden bowls full of *incense, which are the prayers of the saints*. (Revelation 5:8) (emphasis added)

Through Christ We Can Boldly Come to God

The Bible not only exhorts us to come to the throne of God; it admonishes us to come with boldness and confidence. Notice the language of scripture depicting this (emphasis added):

> For through him we both have *access* to the Father by one Spirit. (Ephesians 2:18)

> In him and through faith in him we may *approach* God with *freedom and confidence*. (Ephesians 3:12)

Let us then approach the throne of grace with *confidence*, so that we may receive mercy and find grace to help us in our time of need. (Hebrews 4:16)

Believers' Prayers Affect What is Happening on the Earth

The Bible demonstrates that our prayers are effectual. Our worship of God impacts what is happening on the earth. We know that we have access to His throne. We pray because God has ordained that our prayers be a part of His process in affecting what happens around us. The altar of incense symbolizes the prayers of the saints, interceding for this planet. Jesus instructs His disciples to pray that the kingdom of God express itself on earth. They were to ask for heaven to manifest itself in their very lives: "This, then, is how you should pray: 'Our Father in heaven, hallowed be your name, *your kingdom come, your will be done on earth as it is in heaven*'" (Matthew 6:9–10; emphasis added).

In a vivid depiction of how the prayers of the saints affect our world, John describes that when the prayers of the redeemed literally came to the altar of incense in heaven, this resulted in a powerful response hurled back to the earth:

> Another angel, who had a golden censer, came and stood at the altar. He was given much incense to offer, *with the prayers of all the saints, on the golden altar* before the throne. The smoke of the incense, together with the prayers of the saints, went up before God from the angel's hand. Then the angel took the censer, filled it with fire from the altar, and *hurled it on the earth*; and there came peals of thunder, rumblings, flashes of lightning and an earthquake. (Revelation 8:3–5; emphasis added).

No Strange Incense or Fire on the Altar

The instructions to Moses regarding the ingredients used to make the incense and limitations regarding the offerings to be used on the altar were clear and inviolable. Incense was to be created God's way, not man's. Acceptance before the throne of God was not to have the taint of any fleshly endeavor (emphasis added):

> *Do not offer on this altar any other incense* or any burnt offering or grain offering, and do not pour a drink offering on it. (Exodus 30:9)

> Then the LORD said to Moses, "Take fragrant spices—gum resin, onycha and galbanum—and pure frankincense, all in equal amounts, and make a fragrant blend of incense, the work of a perfumer. It is to be salted and pure and sacred. Grind some of it to powder and place it in front of the Testimony in the Tent of Meeting, where I will meet with you. It shall be most holy to you. *Do not make any incense with this formula for yourselves*; consider it holy to the LORD. *Whoever makes any like it to enjoy its fragrance must be cut off from his people.*" (Exodus 30:34)

In the same fashion, strange fire was forbidden to be used on the altar as well. To ignite the coals on the altar of incense, the fire had to ultimately come from the altar of sacrifice, which derived its fire directly from God. Strange fire represented fire that came from any other source but the Lord. He was not pleased with those who disobeyed this order. Nadab and Abihu found out the hard way: "Aaron's sons Nadab and Abihu took their censers, put fire in them and added incense; and they offered *unauthorized fire* before the LORD, contrary to his command. So fire came out from the presence of the LORD and consumed them, and *they died before the LORD*" (Leviticus 10:1–2; emphasis added).

All of our prayers and worship offered before the Lord must come by way of the cross, not by human endeavors. We are fragrant to God because of Christ and not because of man. The sons of Aaron violated God's instruction and were killed. Sometimes, we are prone to look to the world to ignite the fire in the church and in our lives. True fire that is effectual and lasting needs to come from the Lord.

The Continual Burning of Incense

The incense was required to burn continually to represent the believer's constant acceptance before the Lord. "Aaron must burn fragrant incense on the altar *every morning* when he tends the lamps. He must burn incense again when he lights the lamps at twilight so incense will *burn regularly* before the LORD for the generations to come" (Exodus 30:7–8; emphasis added).

What a wonderful picture of the perpetual intercession the Lord does for us before the throne of God: "Therefore he is able to save completely those who come to God through him, because he *always* lives to intercede for them" (Hebrews 7:25; emphasis added).

This altar also symbolizes the fact that prayer and worship will always be offered to God from the earth in some form. We are admonished to pray continually as a part of our lifestyle as priests before God: "Pay *continually*" (1 Thessalonians 5:17; emphasis added).

It is encouraging and reassuring to know that no matter how dark our world appears to be on this earth, there will always be an expression of prayer and worship lifted to the throne of God by His redeemed church. In fact, the book of Revelation gives us a glimpse in heaven, where there is continuous adoration and praise before the throne of God. What we do on earth is a reflection of heaven: "Each of the four living creatures…and night they *never stop* saying: 'Holy, holy, holy is the Lord God Almighty, who was, and is, and is to come'" (Revelation 4:8) and "Therefore, they are before the throne of God and serve him *day and night* in his temple; and he who sits on the throne will spread his tent over them" (Revelation 7:15). (emphasis added)

Two Altars Compared

Our journey through the tabernacle to this point has led us to two very important altars: the bronze altar and the altar of incense. In many ways, these two altars were polar opposites in their meaning and effects.

Altar of Sacrifice Altar of Incense

Pictures death	Pictures life
Represents the sinner	Represents the saint
Grants us forgiveness before God	Grants us acceptance/access to God
We are brought near	We are kept near
Establishes our worthiness	Establishes our worship
Was a place of penalty	Was a place of prayer

The Altar of Incense

DISCUSSION QUESTIONS

1. Discuss the relationship between Hebrews 7:25 and the meaning of the altar of incense. What application does this have for the believer today?
2. Demonstrate from the New Testament why the believer can now come boldly before the throne of God. How is this different than what we understand from the Old Testament?
3. Why was no strange fire allowed on the altar of incense? Give an example of how strange fire might be offered today?
4. Where in the New Testament do we see this altar in action? How does apply to us today?

9

The Veil of Separation

One of the most fascinating aspects of the tabernacle was the veil of separation placed between the holy of holies and the holy place. Rabbinical records tell us that this veil was several feet thick, and that two teams of oxen could not tear it apart. The veil, like other aspects of the tabernacle, was a picture of Christ and the plan of salvation.

A Multicolored Curtain

In Exodus 26:31–33, specific instructions are given for the construction of this curtain:

> Make a *curtain of blue, purple and scarlet yarn and finely twisted linen,* with *cherubim worked into it* by a skilled craftsman. Hang it with gold hooks on four posts of acacia wood overlaid with gold and standing on four silver bases. Hang the curtain from the clasps and place the ark of the Testimony behind the curtain. *The curtain will separate the Holy Place from the Most Holy Place.* (emphasis added)

The veil was to be multicolored. These are the same colors used in the curtain at the east gate and on the inner covering of the tabernacle. Each color portrayed a certain aspect about Christ and corresponded with one of the four Gospels.

- Purple. Royalty: Jesus the King (Gospel of Matthew)
- Red. Blood: Jesus the Suffering Servant (Gospel of Mark)

- White. Purity: Jesus the Perfect Man (Gospel of Luke)
- Blue. Heaven: Jesus the Son of God (Gospel of John)

The Bible explains that the curtain also had symbols of cherubim worked into it, just like the inner covering. Cherubim were guardians of the holiness of the Lord and represented His righteousness and demand for justice. The combination of colors and cherubim are important. The presence of cherubim indicated that man, because of his sin, was not worthy to come into the holy of holies and experience the presence of Jehovah. The colors displayed God's plan of salvation through Jesus Christ, the only One who could rectify the unworthiness and unholiness of mankind.

A Representation of Jesus's Perfect Humanity

The veil sent the message that one had to be perfect to enter into the holy of holies. It represented perfect righteousness, which could only be found in Christ. The book of Hebrews tells us that this curtain was a picture of Christ's body: "By a new and living way opened for us through the *curtain, that is, his body*" (Hebrews 10:20; emphasis added).

Only Jesus could remove the veil and open the way to God. He was the perfect human being, and, because of that, the only one who could provide the way of salvation. He accomplished this on the cross: "God made him *who had no sin* to be sin for us, so that in him we might become the righteousness of God" (2 Corinthians 5:21) and "Salvation is found in no one else, for there is *no other name* under heaven given to men by which we must be saved" (Acts 4:12). (emphasis added)

A Reminder of Man's Sinfulness

The veil represented Jesus. The curtain clearly revealed that one had to be totally righteous to get into God's presence. Conversely, it sent the message to all mankind that they were not good enough to get in. The veil was a giant "keep out" sign, reminding humanity of his sinfulness. This is why the cherubim were woven into the fabric. The only person who was allowed inside the veil was the high priest, and he went in only once a year. Even the high priest had to shed animal blood for his own sins. This is what the book of Hebrews is talking about in the following verse:

> But only the high priest entered the inner room, and that only *once a year*, and never without blood, which *he offered for himself* and for the sins the people had committed in ignorance. The Holy Spirit was showing by this that the way into the Most Holy Place had not yet been disclosed as long as the first Tabernacle was still standing. (Hebrews 9:7; emphasis added)

The veil in the Old Testament tabernacle was conveying that salvation was not complete because man's sinfulness had not been dealt with fully. Scripture declares that before one comes to Christ, he is an enemy of God, alienated from the Father in every way, dead in trespasses and sins, and a servant of Satan, the ruler of this dark world (emphasis added):

> For if, when *we were God's enemies*, we were reconciled to him through the death of his Son, how much more, having been reconciled, shall we be saved through his life! (Romans 5:10)

> As for you, you were *dead in your transgressions and sins*, in which you used to live when *you followed the ways of this world and of the ruler of the kingdom of the air*, the spirit who is now at work in those who are disobedient. All of us also lived among them at one time, gratifying the cravings of our sinful nature and following its desires and thoughts. Like the rest, we were by nature objects of wrath. (Ephesians 2:1–3)

Someone had to come and remove the veil so that mankind could receive forgiveness of sins and open the door to a restored relationship with God.

Done Away With by Christ's Death

For hundreds of years, the veil stood as a symbol of the separation between man and God. Who would be perfect enough to come and open the way into the Lord's presence? The answer is simple: Jesus Christ. This is dramatically portrayed by the rending of the veil during our Savior's crucifixion. The tearing apart of this sacred curtain in the temple was truly a miracle: "And when Jesus had cried out again in a loud voice, he gave up his spirit. At that moment the *curtain of the temple was torn in two from top to bottom.* The earth shook and the rocks split" (Matthew 27:50–51; emphasis added).

Scripture makes a point to describe a very important detail in the rending of the veil: it was torn from top to bottom. This act emphasized that God was reaching down to man through Christ, not the other way around. Also, this veil was several inches thick and would have been impossible for someone to go in and tear it open. The rending of this curtain during the death of Christ was a tremendously powerful statement that Jesus had opened up the way into the presence of God. The "keep out" sign was removed. Mankind could now be declared righteous before God. The way into the His presence, which had previously been blocked, was now opened. Christ had finished the work and, through Him, humans could reach the perfection necessary to enter into the glory of the Lord. We have access to the very holy of holies and presence of the living God. This is beautifully expressed by the writer of Hebrews: "We have this hope as an anchor for the soul, firm and secure. It enters the inner sanctuary *behind the curtain,* where Jesus, who went before us, has entered *on our behalf.* He has become a high priest forever, in the order of Melchizedek" (Hebrews 6:19–20; emphasis added).

DISCUSSION QUESTIONS

1. What did the veil between the holy place and the holy of holies symbolically portray? What message was it sending?
2. Discuss the significance between the veil in the Old Testament tabernacle and the rending of the veil in Matthew 27:50–51.
3. Now that the veil has been torn apart, what does this mean for the believer today? What message of hope does this provide to those who are outside of Christ?
4. What was the importance of the veil being torn from top to bottom?

VI

THE HOLY OF HOLIES

10

The Ark of the Covenant

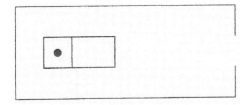

We have come through the courtyard and the holy place and are now ready to discuss the most holy place or the holy of holies. The holy of holies was revered as the most sacred part of the tabernacle. This is where God emphasized His power and presence. The centerpiece of this room was the sacred piece of furniture: the Ark of the Covenant (testimony). It represents many symbolic aspects of Christ and salvation: "Hang the curtain from the clasps and place the *ark of the Testimony* behind the curtain. The curtain will separate the *Holy Place* from the *Most Holy Place*" (Exodus 26:33) and "Behind the second curtain was a room called the Most Holy Place, which had the *gold-covered ark of the covenant*." (Hebrews 9:3–4) (emphasis added)

Acacia Wood and Gold Construction

Moses was given specific instructions for the construction of this chest or ark: "Have them make a chest of *acacia wood*—two and a half cubits long, a cubit and a half wide, and a cubit and a half high. Overlay it with *pure gold*, both inside and out, and make a *gold molding* around it" (Exodus 25:10–11; emphasis added).

True to form, the Ark of the Covenant was constructed of the ubiquitous acacia wood and gold, symbolic of the humanity and deity of Jesus. Salvation would be accomplished through the God-man, Jesus Christ.

One interesting aspect of the Ark was the gold molding to be placed around it. The King James Version translates this as *crown of gold*, establishing a regal aspect to the box. This is another wonderful symbol of Jesus Christ, as He was and still is the King of kings: "On his robe and on his thigh he has this name written: KING OF KINGS and LORD OF LORDS" (Revelation 19:16; emphasis added).

A Box (Ark) of Safety

This box is referred to as an ark. "Then put in the *ark* the Testimony, which I will give you" (Exodus 25:16; emphasis added).

Arks in the Bible were designed for rescue purposes and played a prominent role in the Old Testament. An ark in the form of a boat saved Noah and his family from the flood (Genesis 6–8). Had the Lord not spared Noah and his kin, there would have been no humanity through which the Messiah Jesus would be born. Another use of an ark was when Moses was placed on a river in a basket of bulrushes (KJV translation is *ark*) and was subsequently saved from the wrath of Pharaoh (Exodus chapter 2). Later, Moses would be the one who would deliver Israel from Egypt, allowing his people to become a mighty nation representing God on the earth.

The Ark of the Covenant in the form of a wooden box was located in the holy of holies and, like other arks, is a picture of safety and salvation: Jesus Christ. We are safe in Him. Scripture confirms this: "Who disobeyed long ago when God waited patiently in the days of Noah while the *ark* was being built. In it only a few people, eight in *all, were saved* through water, and this water symbolizes baptism that now saves you also...*It saves you* by the resurrection of Jesus Christ" (1 Peter 3:20–21; emphasis added).

Three Items Inside the Ark

Hebrews 9:4 describes in detail three important items contained in the Ark: "And the gold-covered Ark of the Covenant. This ark contained the *gold jar of manna, Aaron's staff that had budded*, and the *stone tablets of the covenant*" (Hebrews 9:4; emphasis added).

It Contained a Gold Jar of Manna

One of the objects placed inside the Ark of the Covenant was a gold jar of manna. Like the bread on the table in the holy place, the manna was symbolic of Jesus, who came down from heaven to bless and feed His people. Jesus identified Himself with Old Testament manna in His discussions with the Jews:

> Our forefathers ate the manna in the desert; as it is written: "He gave them bread from heaven to eat." Jesus said to them, "I tell you the truth, it is not Moses who has given you the bread from heaven, but it is my Father who gives you *the true bread from heaven*. For the bread of God is he who comes down from heaven and gives life to the world." (John 6:31–33; emphasis added).

In the Bible, bread was a symbol of life and nourishment. Jesus was God's provision for mankind's spiritual life and sustenance. Again, in John 6, Jesus inextricably links the eating of this manna with the receiving of His life: "*I am the living bread* that came down from heaven. *If anyone eats of this bread*, he will live forever. This bread is my flesh, which I will give for the life of the world. *Whoever eats my flesh* and drinks my blood has eternal life and I will raise him up at the last day" (John 6:51, 54; emphasis added).

It Contained Aaron's Rod that had Budded

The second item inside the Ark was Aaron's staff, which had budded. Aaron's rod was an old, dead almond branch incapable of producing any foliage or fruit. Its history is recorded in Numbers:

> So Moses spoke to the Israelites, and their leaders gave him twelve staffs, one for the leader of each of their ancestral tribes, and *Aaron's staff* was among them. Moses placed the staffs before the LORD in the Tent of the Testimony. The next day Moses entered the Tent of the Testimony and saw that Aaron's staff, which represented the house of Levi, had not only sprouted but had budded, *blossomed and produced almonds.* (Numbers 17:6–8; emphasis added).

The historical context of this passage reveals that Israel had been in a state of rebellion against the spiritual leadership of Aaron, the high priest. The Lord used this dead piece of wood to affirm Aaron's leadership. This old stick came to life. Because of this, the people knew that Aaron was the one they were to follow. This is a picture of the resurrection of Christ. He gained His authority to rule in our lives and be our savior by coming back to life from the dead. Because of this, He is the only one who has the authority to provide salvation. New Testament writers are clear and dogmatic that, without the resurrection of Christ, salvation would be an impossibility (emphasis added): "Who was declared the Son of God with power *by the resurrection from the dead,* according to the Spirit of holiness, Jesus Christ our Lord" (Romans 1:4) and "And *if Christ has not been raised, our preaching is useless* and so is your faith…and if Christ has not been raised, your faith is futile; you are still in your sins" (1 Corinthians 15:14, 17; emphasis added).

It Contained the Tablets of the Law

The third item found in the wooden box were stone tablets of the covenant on which the law, or the Ten Commandments, were inscribed by the very finger of God.

> When the LORD finished speaking to Moses on Mount Sinai, he gave him *the two tablets of the Testimony*, the tablets of stone inscribed by the finger of God. (Exodus 31:18)

> There was nothing in the ark except the *two stone tablets that Moses* had placed in it at Horeb, where the LORD made a covenant with the Israelites after they came out of Egypt. (1 Kings 8:9) (emphasis added)

This piece of furniture is called the Ark of the Covenant because of its association with the covenant between Moses and Jehovah, centered around the law. In essence, the Lord would bless and protect Israel if she would obey and love Him. The law was a description of the perfect lifestyle. It was intended to be a guide and pattern for Israel's behavior to reflect her devotion to the Lord. The problem was that no one could keep the law perfectly. In fact, the Bible stresses the purpose of the giving of the law was to expose man's sinfulness and point to its need for a savior:

> What shall we say, then? Is the law sin? Certainly not! Indeed *I would not have known what sin was except through the law.* For I would not have known what coveting really was if the law had not said, "Do not covet." (Romans 7:7)

> Before this faith came, we were held *prisoners by the law*, locked up until faith should be revealed. So *the law was put in charge to lead us to Christ* that we might be justified by faith. Now that faith has come, we are no longer under the supervision of the law. (Galatians 3:23–25) (emphasis added)

The tablets condemned mankind and always pointed to his failure to live up to God's law. This is what the New Testament means when it describes the law as an instructor to show humanity its need for salvation. This is why the tabernacle was constructed in the first place. The tablets were in the Ark as a reminder that Christ was the only one who could fulfill the requirements of the law. Once He came and died, the Mosaic Law would no longer be the standard for New Testament believers' lifestyle. The Lord Jesus Himself would now fulfill that role: "Christ is the *end of the law* so that there may be righteousness for everyone who believes" (Romans 10:4; emphasis added).

The three items in the Ark of the Covenant paint an incredible picture. Jesus, the provisional "manna," came from heaven to earth. He would die and resurrect so that mankind could be delivered from the curse and judgment of the Ten Commandments.

Always Carried by Priests

Another interesting aspect of the Ark is the fact that the carrying poles stayed on it all the time. The reason for this was simple: the Ark was never to be touched or opened up to look inside by any human. This is why it was perpetually to be carried by priests as its mode of transportation and not handled with human hands. "The *poles are to remain in the rings* of this ark; they *are not to be removed*" (Exodus 25:15) and "And he inserted the poles into the rings on the sides of the ark to *carry it*" (Exodus 37:5). (emphasis added)

The movie *Raiders of the Lost Ark*, in Hollywood fashion, demonstrated the tragic results when individuals callously violated this sacred principle of not touching or looking into the Ark of the Covenant. The movie was fictional. However, there are a couple of real-life biblical examples illustrating this as well.

Disaster at Beth-Shemesh

After the Philistines had commandeered the Ark of the Covenant from Israel, they experienced nothing but disaster and misery in the form of tumors, which inflicted all of their geographical regions. Finally, out of sheer exasperation, they placed the Ark on a cart with appropriate penitent sacrifices and brought it to a farming town named Beth-Shemesh, hoping to assuage the judgment of God. The people of Beth-Shemesh worshipped the Lord and offered burnt offerings in celebration of the Ark's return. However, the Lord was not pleased with some of the men in the town, who audaciously violated the sacred honor of the Ark by touching it and peering into its contents: "But God struck down some of the men of Beth Shemesh, putting seventy of them to death *because they had looked into the ark of the* LORD. The people mourned because of the heavy blow the LORD had dealt them" (1 Samuel 6:19; emphasis added).

This was an ominous warning to anyone who would desecrate the Ark in this fashion.

Death Comes to Uzzah

Because of the incident at Beth Shemesh, the people of the town, out of disillusionment and fear, sent messengers to the nearby village of Kiriath Jearim to ask for someone to come and retrieve the Ark from Beth-Shemesh, which they did. The Ark stayed in Kiriath Jearim for twenty years:

> So the men of Kiriath Jearim came and took up the ark of the LORD. They took it to Abinadab's house on the hill and consecrated Eleazar his son to guard the ark of the LORD. It was a long time, *twenty years* in all, that the ark remained at Kiriath Jearim, and all the people of Israel mourned and sought after the LORD. (1 Samuel 7:1–2; emphasis added).

When David became king, he realized the Ark of the Covenant needed to be moved and centered in a more strategic and prominent location: the city of David. After defeating the Philistines, David retrieved the Ark and placed it on a cart to transport it. Along the way, the cart stumbled, putting this precious cargo in the precarious position of falling off. Uzzah, one of David's men assigned to protect the Ark, reached out and touched it to prevent it from falling off the oxen cart as they were transporting it to the city of David. This act cost him his life as he violated the sacredness of the Ark by touching it: "When they came to the threshing floor of Nacon, *Uzzah reached out and took hold of the ark of God*, because the oxen stumbled. The Lord's anger burned against Uzzah because of his irreverent act; therefore *God struck him down* and he died there beside the ark of God" (2 Samuel 6:6–7; emphasis added).

As we have noted, the Ark was never meant or designed to be carried on a cart; it was to be transported by priests. David made the tragic mistake of transporting God's holy box in the same fashion the pagan Philistines had done. If the Ark had been carried by priests in the way God originally designed, Uzzah would not have been in position to touch the Ark and, consequently, pay for this action with his life. David, in fear, anger, and frustration, gave up on transporting the Ark to the City of David, and the Bible reveals it stayed with a man named Obed-Edom for three months, where the Lord abundantly blessed him (2 Samuel 6:10–11). However, having learned his lesson, David went back to Obed-Edom, regained possession of the Ark of the Covenant and transported it correctly this time by making the priests carry it: "When those who were *carrying the ark* of the LORD had taken six steps, he sacrificed a bull and a fattened calf" (2 Samuel 6:13).

The Shekinah glory of God attended this Ark; therefore, it was sacred and holy. It was to be carried by priests while given respect and honor. All of this foreshadowed a coming priesthood, Christ's church, who would carry the glory of God and show it to the world: "To them God has chosen to make known among the Gentiles the glorious riches of this mystery, which is *Christ in you, the hope of glory*" (Colossians 1:27).

The Ark of the Testimony

DISCUSSION QUESTIONS

1. What significant role did arks play in the Old Testament? What did the Ark of the Covenant in the holy of holies ultimately picture?

2. Name some of the ways we can practically eat of the *living manna*, Jesus Christ. How does the bread of life nourish us today?

3. Explain the meaning of Aaron's rod that budded and its symbolism of Christ. Why is the resurrection of Jesus essential for the message of salvation? How does Aaron's budding rod demonstrate Jesus's superior credentials over all other religious founders?

4. Why was it so important that the Ark be carried on the shoulders of priests? How does this symbolize the New Testament church?

5. Is the law of Moses a way of life for New Testament believers? If not, why not, and what usefulness does it play for the New Testament church?

11

The Mercy Seat

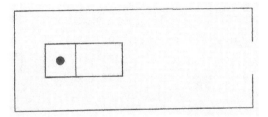

Perhaps the greatest picture of Christ in the tabernacle was the mercy seat or atonement cover, which was placed on top of the Ark of the Covenant as the previous picture illustrates. "Make an *atonement cover* of pure gold—two and a half cubits long and a cubit and a half wide. And make two cherubim out of hammered gold at the ends of the cover" (Exodus 25:17–18; emphasis added).

All of our study has led us to this point. Several aspects of the mercy seat depict Christ and the plan of salvation.

On Top of the Ark Between
the Law and the Cherubim

The mercy seat was to be placed on top of the Ark of the Covenant between the tablets of the law located inside the box, and the cherubim looking down upon it. "Place the *cover on top of the ark* and put in the ark the Testimony, which I will give you" (Exodus 25:21; emphasis added).

The mercy seat of grace was sandwiched between the tablets of law contained in the Ark (which condemned mankind) and the cherubim (who demand justice and judgment). This is the story of salvation: judgment demanded for those who cannot keep the law, while grace is provided in the person of Jesus Christ: "And to wait for his Son from heaven, whom he raised from the dead— Jesus, who *rescues us from the coming wrath*" (1 Thessalonians 1:10; emphasis added).

Pure Gold Construction

The cover was made of pure gold. The gold depicts the innocence and purity of Christ. It also represents His deity. "Make an atonement cover of *pure gold*—two and a half cubits long and a cubit and a half wide" (Exodus 25:17; emphasis added).

Jesus was the most innocent individual ever to be executed. The Bible declares that He was sinless, which stood in contrast to the depraved condition of the human race for whom He died: "He made Him who knew no sin to be sin on our behalf, that we might become the righteousness of God in Him" (2 Corinthians 5:21).

Two Cherubim of Hammered Gold

Attached to the ends of the mercy seat were two cherubim (high-level spirit beings) made from hammered gold. These spirit beings are very important to the meaning of the mercy seat. "And make *two cherubim* out of *hammered gold* at the ends of the cover" (Exodus 25:18) and "Above the ark were the *cherubim* of the Glory, overshadowing the atonement cover. But we cannot discuss these things in detail now (Hebrews 9:5; emphasis added).

Christ Beaten

The fact that the cherubim were forged from hammered gold symbolized the fact that Christ had to be beaten unto death to become our mercy seat and receive the judgment upon Himself, which we deserved. This is what the prophet was referring to in his description of the suffering Messiah: "Surely he took up our infirmities and carried our sorrows, yet we considered him stricken by God, smitten by him, and afflicted. But he was *pierced* for our transgressions, he was *crushed* for our iniquities; the *punishment* that brought us peace was upon him, and by his *wounds* we are healed" (Isaiah 53:4–5; emphasis added).

Demanding Judgment

The cherubim were continually looking down on the Ark of the Covenant and the mercy seat. These creatures were the guardians of God's purposes. They executed His judgments. Their role is defined in the Garden of Eden as they enforced the punishment God had pronounced on the human race: "After he drove the man out, he placed on the east side of the Garden of Eden *cherubim* and a flaming sword flashing back and forth to *guard the way* to the tree of life" (Genesis 3:24; emphasis added).

David describes the majesty of God by using the figure of cherubim: "He mounted the *cherubim* and flew; he soared on the wings of the wind" (Psalm 18:10; emphasis added).

The cherubim were also incorporated into the tapestry of the veil, where their presence reminded mankind of his sin. As these creatures look down on the Ark of the Covenant and the law it contains, their presence cries out for judgment on those who cannot keep the law. Fortunately, in the presence of the mercy seat, there is an object that can satisfy their demands for justice.

A Place of Annual Blood Atonement

The mercy seat was also known as the *atonement cover*. Upon this cover is where the high priest placed the blood of the sacrificed animals:

> Make an *atonement cover* of pure gold—two and a half cubits long and a cubit and a half wide. (Exodus 25:17)

> Once a year Aaron shall make *atonement* on its horns. This *annual atonement* must be made with the *blood of the atoning sin offering* for the generations to come. It is most holy to the LORD. (Exodus 30:10)

> He is to take some of the bull's *blood* and with his finger sprinkle it on the front of the *atonement* cover; then he shall sprinkle some of it with his finger seven times before the *atonement cover*. (Leviticus 16:14)

> In this way he will make *atonement* for the Most Holy Place because of the uncleanness and rebellion of the Israelites, whatever their sins have been. He is to do the same for the Tent of Meeting, which is among them in the midst of their uncleanness. (Leviticus 16:16) (emphasis added)

The word *atonement* in the Hebrew, *kāphar*, essentially means *to cover*. This is why the Jewish holy day is called *Yom Kippur*, or the Day of Atonement. On this day, Israel's sins would be covered or atoned for one year because of the blood applied to the mercy seat. A verbal form of *kāphar* is used in Genesis 6:14, where Noah is instructed to *coat* or *cover* the ark with pitch to prevent the water from coming into the boat. This may be the first tacit reference to the relationship between atonement and salvation.

Moses, who was imparted these instructions, was very familiar with the power of blood to save. Prior to the Exodus of Israel from Egypt, the Lord gave specific instructions to him concerning the blood, which would eventually spare Israel the fate of the Egyptians:

Then they are to take some of the *blood* and put it on the sides and tops of the doorframes of the houses where they eat the lambs…"On that same night I will pass through Egypt and strike down every firstborn—both men and animals—and I will bring judgment on all the gods of Egypt. I am the LORD. The blood will be a sign for you on the houses where you are; and *when I see the blood, I will pass over you.* No destructive plague will touch you when I strike Egypt." (Exodus 12:7, 12–13; emphasis added).

In the same way that the blood applied to the Jewish homes in Egypt saved them from death, the blood applied to the mercy seat in the tabernacle would spare them from God's judgment for their sins. The limitation with this mercy seat was that it only covered Israel's sins for one year. This is why the book of Hebrews makes it clear that the blood sacrifice of animals was inferior to the ultimate sacrifice made by Jesus Christ: "But those sacrifices are an *annual reminder* of sins, because it is impossible for the blood of bulls and goats to take away sins" (Hebrews 10:3–4; emphasis added).

I will discuss the importance of atonement in detail in chapter 14.

Christ: Our Mercy Seat

The New Testament is unequivocal: Christ is the ultimate fulfillment of the mercy seat. "God presented *him* as a *sacrifice of atonement* [mercy seat], through faith in his blood. He did this to demonstrate his justice, because in his forbearance he had left the sins committed beforehand unpunished" (Romans 3:25; emphasis added).

The word *atonement* in this verse is the Greek word *hilastarion*, which literally means *mercy seat* or *the place where sins are forgiven*. It is also used in Hebrews 9:5 to describe the mercy seat or atonement cover in the Old Testament. The King James renders the translation of *hilastarion* as *propitiation*, meaning Christ's death has satisfied God's judgment for our sin. In this verse, Paul is teaching that Christ is the equivalent and fulfillment of the mercy seat in the Old Testament tabernacle. The writer of Hebrews echoes the same idea:

"He did not enter by means of the blood of goats and calves; but he entered the Most Holy Place once for all *by his own blood*, having obtained eternal redemption" (Hebrews 9:12; emphasis added).

The high priest was required to make atonement for sins annually, but Christ only had to do it once. When Christ entered the heavenly holy of holies, He offered His blood and then sat down—salvation and forgiveness were final. "But when this priest had offered for all time *one sacrifice for sins*, he *sat down* at the right hand of God" (Hebrews 10:12; emphasis added).

The Gospels give us insight into this process. After Jesus was resurrected and subsequently showed Himself to Mary Magdalene, she proceeded to try and enthusiastically embrace Him, but He refrained her from holding on to Him, offering the reason that He had to return to the Father: "Jesus said, *Do not hold on to me*, for *I have not yet returned to the Father*. Go instead to my brothers and tell them, 'I am returning to my Father and your Father, to my God and your God'" (John 20:17; emphasis added).

However, later that evening, Jesus appears to His disciples and encourages them to touch Him: "Look at my hands and my feet. It is I myself! *Touch me and see*; a ghost does not have flesh and bones, as you see I have" (Luke 24:39; emphasis added).

What a difference from earlier in the day to evening! Why would Jesus forbid Mary from touching Him when, merely hours later, He welcomes the disciples to do so? The answer may well lay in the statement Jesus made to Mary that He had to return to His Father. Remember, in the Old Testament, before the high priest had interaction with anyone, he had to place the blood on the mercy seat and complete his responsibilities on the Day of Atonement. It could be that when Jesus met Mary, He had not returned to heaven to place His blood on the mercy seat of heaven and, sometime between His encounter with her earlier in the day and His meeting with the disciples that evening, it was accomplished.

After the resurrection, His first duty as high priest was to atone for sin and secure salvation. After that was accomplished,

He would be free to have interaction with His followers who had just been purchased by His blood. Jesus had now totally fulfilled the symbol of the mercy seat and insured by a new covenant that blood would never have to be shed again for the forgiveness of sins: "To Jesus the mediator of a *new covenant*, and to *the sprinkled blood* that speaks a better word than the blood of Abel" (Hebrews 12:24; emphasis added).

DISCUSSION QUESTIONS

1. What is the relationship between the tablets of the law contained in the ark and the presence of cherubim over the mercy seat?

2. What is the significance of the cherubim being made of hammered gold?

3. Discuss Romans 3:25 and the meaning of the mercy seat as it relates to Christ. What is the main difference between the mercy seat in the Old Testament and the New Testament?

4. What does the mercy seat convey to us about the nature of God?

12

The Glory of God

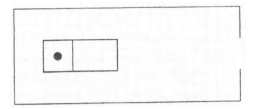

The last item to be discussed with regard to the holy of holies is the glory of God. The Jews referred to this glory as the Shekinah glory, expressing the resident presence of Jehovah. Our first exposure to the glory of God was in the Garden of Eden. We are told that before the Fall, Adam and Eve were naked and unashamed (Genesis 2:25). Something was covering their bodies that apparently left after they sinned. It was probably the glory and presence of God that left them, and they were now ashamed and naked as they saw themselves as fallen humanity stripped of God's glory.

Israel experienced this powerful glory after leaving Egypt, as the Lord guided his people by means of a cloud by day and fire by night. "After leaving Succoth they camped at Etham on the edge of the desert. By day the LORD went ahead of them in a *pillar of cloud* to guide them on their way and by night in a *pillar of fire* to give them light, so that they could travel by day or night" (Exodus 13:20–21; emphasis added).

Moses was intimately familiar with this dynamic glory. After meeting with God on Mount Sinai, his face reflected the light and glory of God's presence. The New Testament reveals to us something about this glory. The glory on Moses was a fading glory, later to be replaced by the glory of Christ, which would last forever:

> When Moses went up on the mountain, the cloud covered it, and *the glory of the* LORD settled on Mount Sinai. For six days the cloud covered the mountain, and on the seventh day the LORD called to Moses from within the cloud. To the Israelites *the glory of the* LORD looked like a consuming fire on top of the mountain. (Exodus 24:15–17)

> For what was glorious has no glory now in comparison with the surpassing *glory*. And if what was fading away came with glory, how much greater is the *glory* of that which lasts! Therefore, since we have such a hope, we are very bold. We are not like Moses, who would put a veil over his face to keep the Israelites from gazing at it while the *radiance was fading away*. (2 Corinthians 3:10–13) (emphasis added)

Resident in the Tabernacle

The Shekinah glory of God in the Old Testament was specifically associated with the tabernacle, more specifically the holy of holies. We have a vivid description of this in Exodus, as the glory of God descended upon the tabernacle:

> Then the cloud covered the *Tent of Meeting*, and the *glory of the* LORD *filled the Tabernacle*. Moses could not enter the Tent of Meeting because the cloud had settled upon it and the glory of the LORD filled the Tabernacle. In all the travels of the Israelites, whenever the cloud lifted from above the Tabernacle, they would set out; but if the cloud did not lift, they did not set out—until the day it lifted. (Exodus 40:34–37; emphasis added).

The Tabernacle would evolve much later into a more elaborate and permanent structure called the temple. When Solomon finished building the temple, the same Shekinah glory came upon it as it did the tabernacle.

The trumpeters and singers joined in unison, as with one voice, to give praise and thanks to the LORD. Accompanied by trumpets, cymbals and other instruments, they raised their voices in praise to the LORD and sang: "He is good; his love endures forever." Then the temple of the LORD was filled with a cloud and the priests could not perform their service because of the cloud, for the *glory of the* LORD *filled the temple of God.* (2 Chronicles 5:13–14; emphasis added).

A Sign of God's Presence

The tabernacle was where God emphasized His presence. In essence, it was where He lived on the earth. It is hard for our limited human minds to process how God could abide somewhere on earth, since He is an immense Spirit and invisible. But God can choose to focus His manifestation anywhere He desires. Later, when the tabernacle evolved into the temple, Solomon even wondered how God, who is so great, could live in the temple he was going to build:

The temple I am going to build will be great, because our God is greater than all other gods. But who is able to build a temple for him, *since the heavens, even the highest heavens, cannot contain him?* Who then am I to build a temple for him, except as a place to burn sacrifices before him? (2 Chronicles 2:5–6; emphasis added).

In the Old Testament, the Jews looked upon this tent as the house of God, and the glory of God represented His presence, power, and residence. Later, Haggai refers to the temple as the house of God:

This is what the LORD Almighty says: "These people say, 'The time has not yet come for the LORD's *house* to be built.' Then the word of the LORD came through the prophet Haggai. (Haggai 1:2–3)

You expected much, but see, it turned out to be little. What you brought home, I blew away. Why?" declares the LORD

Almighty. "Because of *my house*, which remains a ruin, while each of you is busy with his own house." (Haggai 1:9) (emphasis added)

A Powerful Force, Focused in the Ark

One of the saddest moments in Israel's history was when, because of her egregious sins and wanton disregard of her sacred relationship to Jehovah, the glory of God departed from Israel after the Philistines captured the Ark. This was devastating, since the power Israel needed to fight her battles effectively was associated with the glory of God contained in the Ark. "So the Philistines fought, and the *Israelites were defeated* and every man fled to his tent. The slaughter was very great; Israel lost thirty-thousand foot soldiers. *The ark of God was captured*, and Eli's two sons, Hophni and Phinehas, died" (1 Samuel 4:10–11; emphasis added).

To reflect this tragedy, Eli's daughter-in-law named her son *Ichabod*, meaning *no glory*. "She named the boy Ichabod, saying, '*The glory has departed from Israel*'—*because of the capture of the ark of God* and the deaths of her father-in-law and her husband" (1 Samuel 4:21; emphasis added).

Without the glory of God resident in the Ark of the Covenant, Israel was no match for her enemies. She was, in essence, an ordinary people like any other nation.

Required, a Perfect Dimension

The glory of God, which represented God's power and presence, resided in the holy of holies. The glory was not associated with the courtyard or the holy place. The dimensions of the holy of holies were unique and demonstrate why God emphasized His presence and power there and not in the other parts of the Tabernacle.

The Holy of Holies was a Perfect Cube

The dimensions of the holy of holies reveal that it was a cube. It was long as it was wide and high. A cube is considered a perfectly sized shape. This point is important, since God can only dwell in perfection. Notice the cubic dimensions of the holy of holies:

> He prepared the inner sanctuary within the temple to set the Ark of the Covenant of the LORD there. The inner sanctuary was *twenty cubits long, twenty wide* and *twenty high*. He overlaid the inside with pure gold, and he also overlaid the altar of cedar. (1 Kings 6:19–20)

> And he measured the length of the inner sanctuary; it was *twenty* cubits, and its width was *twenty* cubits across the end of the outer sanctuary. He said to me, "This is the Most Holy Place." (Ezekiel 41:4) (emphasis added)

A cubit is about eighteen inches in our dimensions, or a foot-and-a-half. The holy of holies was indeed a cube.

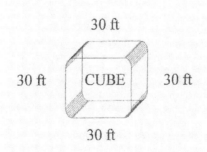

This cubical form symbolized the point that God would only dwell in a place that was perfect. This foreshadowed the two other perfect places, which would become the residence of God's glory: Jesus Christ and His church.

Jesus Christ was the Holy of Holies in Human Form

We have noted that the glory or presence of God abided in the holy of holies of the Old Testament tabernacle. The dimensions symbolize a place of perfection—the only place suitable for the presence of God. Similarly, the New Testament reveals that Jesus Christ Himself was inhabited by this same glory, thus fulfilling the symbolism of the Old Testament: "The Word became flesh and made his *dwelling* among us. We have seen *his glory*, the glory of the One and Only, who came from the Father, full of grace and truth" (John 1:14; emphasis added).

Jesus was, in essence, a human tabernacle (holy of holies) inhabited by the glory of God. His body was a place of perfection. When one saw Jesus, he saw the presence and power of God. Just as the holy of holies represented perfection by its dimensions, Jesus Christ represented perfect humanity by His sinlessness: "God made him *who had no sin* to be sin for us, so that in him we might become the righteousness of God" (2 Corinthians 5:21; emphasis added).

The Holy of Holies is God's Church Today

The Old Testament holy of holies would eventually appear not only in the person of Jesus Christ, but also in His church. The church, His resident body today, is God's holy of holies. We are where God lives on the earth. In several ways, the New Testament defines the people of God as the present-day holy of holies.

Paul Refers to Church as the Temple of God

Paul states unequivocally that the church is now the temple of God, the present-day holy of holies:

> Don't you know that you yourselves are God's *temple* and that God's Spirit lives in you? (1 Corinthians 3:16)

> Do you not know that your *body is a temple* of the Holy Spirit, who is in you, whom you have received from God? You are not your own. (1 Corinthians 6:19)

In Him the whole building is joined together and rises to become a *holy temple* in the Lord. And in Him you too are being built together to become a dwelling in which *God lives by his Spirit*. (Ephesians 2:21–22) (emphasis added)

In the New Testament, two primary Greek words for temple are commonly used. The first is *hieros*, which means *a temple in general*. The second word is *naos*, which denotes *the inner temple* or *the holy of holies*. In fact, this word is used exclusively by Paul to refer to the church (1 Corinthians 3:16, 17; 2 Corinthians 6:16; Ephesians 2:21; and 2 Thessalonians 2:4). This confirms what Paul stated to the philosophers on Mars Hill concerning the relationship between God and physical temples: "The God who made the world and everything in it is the Lord of heaven and earth and *does not live in temples built by hands*" (Acts 17:24; emphasis added).

God does not dwell in man-made temples because He has chosen to live in human temples, His redeemed church. Just as Jesus fulfilled the symbolism of the Old Testament glory, the church is continuing to fulfill it now.

Paul States That The Glory Dwells in Us

Paul also indicates the church is God's present-day holy of holies by stating the glory of God dwells in us: "To them God has chosen to make known among the Gentiles the glorious riches of this mystery, which is *Christ in you, the hope of glory*" (Colossians 1:27; emphasis added).

The church is the representation of the power and presence of God on earth. In contrast to the glory associated with Moses, the church possesses an ever-increasing glory. God's presence and power will continue to grow in expression and power as long as the church is on earth. This is the essence of the Apostle Paul's instruction to the Corinthian church: "And *we*, who with unveiled faces all reflect the Lord's glory, are being transformed into his likeness with *ever-increasing glory*, which comes from the Lord, who is the Spirit" (2 Corinthians 3:18).

Paul affirms that the Spirit of God, representing Jesus, now lives in us. Paul makes it very clear that the Holy Spirit, who is the third person of the trinity and the very essence of God, now dwell in us: "But if Christ is in you, your body is dead because of sin, yet your spirit is alive because of righteousness. And if the Spirit of him who raised Jesus from the dead is living in you, He who raised Christ from the dead will also give life to your mortal bodies through *His Spirit, who lives in you*" (Romans 8:10–11, emphasis added).

This affirms what Jesus related to His disciples when He was with them: "The *Spirit of truth*. The world cannot accept Him, because it neither sees Him nor knows Him. But you know Him, for He lives with you and *will be in you*" (John 14:17, emphasis added).

It cannot be any clearer. Because the Spirit of God inhabits the church, the church is indwelt by the glory of God. John describes the church with perfect dimensions, just as the holy of holies was described in the Old Testament.

In the New Testament, one of the metaphors for the church is the city called *the New Jerusalem*. This city of God is a description of the church. We know this because John describes this city as the bride of the Lamb:

> I saw the Holy City, *the New Jerusalem*, coming down out of heaven from God, prepared as *a bride* beautifully dressed for her husband. (Revelation 21:2)

> One of the seven angels who had the seven bowls full of the seven last plagues came and said to me, "Come, I will show you *the bride, the wife of the Lamb*." And he carried me away in the Spirit to a mountain great and high, and showed me *the Holy City, Jerusalem*, coming down out of heaven from God. (Revelation 21:9–10) (emphasis added)

It is also interesting that when John describes the dimensions of the New Jerusalem, he depicts it as a perfect cube, in the same way the Old Testament characterized the tabernacle's holy of holies as a perfect cube: "The city was laid out like a square, as long as it was wide. He measured the city with the rod and found it to be *12,000 stadia in length, and as wide and high as it is long*" (Revelation 21:16; emphasis added).

John lays out the length, width, and height of the city as a cube of twelve thousand stadia. The number *12* in the book of Revelation is symbolic of God's church. This perfect dimension was used by design since God can only dwell in that which is without blemish. The church fulfills, by its perfect dimensions, the Old Testament holy of holies.

Because of Christ, the Church is Declared Perfect and Blameless Before God

Some may have difficulty seeing how the church can be described as perfect, since even a cursory glance at many followers of Christ divulges a myriad of imperfections. When we refer to the church as perfect, we are speaking about her *positional* standing before God. Because of Christ, we stand before Him blameless and perfect. The Bible says:

> It is because of him that you are in Christ Jesus, who has become for us wisdom from God—that is, our *righteousness, holiness* and redemption. (1 Corinthians 1:30)

> God made him who had no sin to be sin for us, so that in him *we might become* the *righteousness of God*. (2 Corinthians 5:21)

> For he chose us in him before the creation of the world to be *holy* and *blameless* in his sight. (Ephesians 1:4) (emphasis added)

Because of Jesus's work on the cross, God has forgiven and cleansed us from all sin and unrighteousness. We have a perfect, righteous standing before the Father. Therefore, God can choose to live in us. The Old Testament holy of holies represented perfection.

Later, Jesus reflected that same flawlessness. Now the church fulfills it as well. All three meet the requirement of perfection required to be the dwelling place of God's glory.

DISCUSSION QUESTIONS

1. What did the glory of God represent in the Old Testament? Why was this important for Israel?
2. Discuss the dimensions of the holy of holies. Why did the holy of holies have to be a cube?
3. Where is the holy of holies on earth today? Support this from scripture.
4. How can the church be described as blameless, when it is evident that we still have faults and imperfections?

VII

The High Priest

13

His Description

A study of the tabernacle would be incomplete without a thorough discussion of the high priest. The high priest played a key role in the tabernacle and in the nation's worship. Both Old and New Testaments contribute much to this topic. To thoroughly appreciate the role and function of the high priest, a few questions must be asked.

Who Was He?

In general, the priests were in charge of Israel's worship and religious, spiritual service to God. The high priest was the overseer of all other priests. He was the only person allowed to enter the holy presence of God in the most holy place/holy of holies on the Day of Atonement. The high priest represented the people before the Lord and made sacrifices and offerings on their behalf. The book of Hebrews gives us a clear definition of the function of the high priest (emphasis added):

> Every *high priest* is selected from among men and is *appointed to represent them* in matters related to God, to offer gifts and sacrifices for sins. (Hebrews 5:1)

> Unlike the other high priests, he does not need *to offer sacrifices* day after day, first for his own sins, and then for the sins of the people. He sacrificed for their sins once for all when he offered himself. (Hebrews 7:27)

Israel's first high priest was Aaron, the brother of Moses. Aaron and his sons came from the tribe of Levi (Exodus 6:16–20). "Have *Aaron* your brother brought to you from among the Israelites, along with his sons Nadab and Abihu, Eleazar and Ithamar, so they may serve me as *priests*" (Exodus 28:1) and "And put headbands on them. Then tie sashes on *Aaron* and his sons. The *priesthood is theirs by a lasting ordinance*. In this way you shall ordain Aaron and his sons" (Exodus 29:9). (emphasis added)

Aaron, the high priest, symbolized the coming of another high priest, Jesus Christ:

> Unlike the other *high priests, he* [Jesus] does not need to offer sacrifices day after day, first for his own sins, and then for the sins of the people. He sacrificed for their sins once for all when he offered himself. For the law appoints as high priests men who are weak; but the oath, which came after the law, appointed the Son, who has been made perfect forever. (Hebrews 7:27–28; emphasis added).

In the same way, the Old Testament high priest was in charge of all other priests. Jesus, the New Testament high priest, is over all priests who are members of God's family.

What Did He Wear?

The esteemed position of the high priest was reflected in his clothing. In Exodus 28, seven pieces of the high priest's attire are mentioned. These garments are called sacred garments. Seven is the perfect number, looking ahead to the perfect high priest, Jesus Christ. Each piece of clothing is adorned with rich symbolism.

He Wore Linen Undergarments

"Make *linen undergarments* as a covering for the body, reaching from the waist to the thigh" (Exodus 28:42; emphasis added).

Linen was a very fine white fabric. It was a practical material but not ornate or fancy. These undergarments were worn in the everyday life of the high priest and were the closest to his body. As we discussed under our treatment of the linen curtains on the outside of the main fence, fine white linen represents perfect righteousness and purity. Jesus, in His everyday life, was perfect. This is why He could be our high priest: "God made him who *had no sin* to be sin for us, so that in him we might become the righteousness of God" (2 Corinthians 5:21; emphasis added).

The linen undergarments also provided a practical function for the high priest: they limited his sweating. One of the interesting aspects concerning the priest's service to God was that he was not allowed to sweat. This is why he wore linen:

> "But the priests, who are Levites and descendants of Zadok and who faithfully carried out the duties of my sanctuary when the Israelites went astray from me, are to come near to minister before me; they are to stand before me to offer sacrifices of fat and blood," declares the Sovereign LORD. "They alone are to enter my sanctuary; they alone are to come near my table to minister before me and perform my service. When they enter the gates of the inner court, they are to wear linen clothes; they must not wear any woolen garment while ministering at the gates of the inner court or inside the temple. They are to wear linen turbans on their heads and linen undergarments around their waists. *They must not wear anything that makes them perspire.*" (Ezek. 44:15–18; emphasis added)

By forbidding His priests to sweat, God was sending the message that worship and ministry to the Lord was not to be done in the atmosphere of human work and effort. Worship was to proceed from God's anointing, not sweat reflecting man-made endeavors.

He Wore a Linen Tunic

"Weave the *tunic of fine linen* and make the turban of fine linen. The sash is to be the work of an embroiderer" (Exodus 28:39; emphasis added).

The tunic was a coat that reached down to the high priest's feet. It also was made of fine linen and covered his whole body. This tunic and the undergarments were not the clothes of majesty or beauty. They were his everyday, ordinary attire. The tunic, like the undergarments, pointed toward the purity of Jesus Christ, the coming high priest.

He Wore a Robe

> Make the *robe of the ephod* entirely of blue cloth, with an opening for the head in its center. There shall be a woven edge like a collar around this opening, so that it will not tear. Make *pomegranates* of blue, purple and scarlet yarn around the hem of the robe, with *gold bells* between them. The gold bells and the pomegranates are to alternate around the hem of the robe. Aaron must wear it when he ministers. The sound of the bells will be heard when he enters the Holy Place before the LORD and when he comes out, so that he will not die. (Exodus 28:31–35; emphasis added)

The robe was worn over the tunic and made of blue cloth. Blue is the symbol of heaven. The high priest had an appointment from above. Later, Jesus, the true high priest, would leave heaven to minister on the earth.

The robe was worn over the linen undergarments and tunic. It was adorned with pomegranates of blue, purple, and scarlet on the bottom hem, alternating between gold bells. The pomegranates served a very functional purpose as they kept the bells from making too much noise. The colors of the pomegranates are symbolic for heaven, royalty, and blood. Our high priest would come from heaven, in the person of Jesus Christ to be our king and sacrifice His life for us.

The golden bells also served a very important function. It was imperative on the Day of Atonement that the high priest perform his duties flawlessly before the presence of the Lord, lest he die. Tradition has it that, on the Day of Atonement, a rope was attached to the high priest. If the high priest died while in the holy of holies, the other priests could pull him out by the rope. When the high priest put back on his robe in the holy place, the tinkling of the bells told the other priests that the high priest was still alive.

The pomegranates and bells symbolically also may show the balance between character and works in the life of the high priest. Paul certainly uses the ideas of fruit and noise to metaphorically show the balance between character and gifts in 1 Corinthians 13:1, when he discusses the relationship between love and spiritual gifts.

He Wore an Ephod

> Make the *ephod of gold,* and of *blue, purple* and *scarlet yarn,* and of *finely twisted linen*—the work of a skilled craftsman… Take *two onyx stones* and engrave on them the *names of the sons of Israel*…and fasten them on the shoulder pieces of the ephod as memorial stones for the sons of Israel. Aaron is to bear the names on his shoulders as a memorial before the LORD. (Exodus 28:6, 9, 12; emphasis added).

Over the robe, the priest wore a sleeveless jacket called an ephod. This ephod contained all of the colors used in the robe, which foreshadowed Jesus Christ. On two onyx stones, the names of the tribes of Israel were engraved and placed on the shoulders of the ephod. Shoulders represent responsibility and strength. The high priest carried the burdens of the whole nation on his shoulders. This symbolism points to Christ, who carried the burden of our salvation on His shoulders as well. He represents the whole church before our God, and He is strong on our behalf: "But because Jesus lives forever, he has a permanent priesthood. Therefore he is able to *save completely* those who come to God through him, because he always *lives to intercede* for them" (Hebrews 7:24–25; emphasis added).

He Wore a Breastplate

> Fashion a *breastpiece* for making decisions—the work of a skilled craftsman. Make it like the ephod: of gold, and of blue, purple and scarlet yarn, and of finely twisted linen. It is to be square—a span long and a span wide—and folded double. (Exodus 28:15–16)

> There are to be *twelve stones*, one for each of the names of the sons of Israel, each engraved like a seal with the name of one of the *twelve tribes*. (Exodus 28:21)

> Whenever Aaron enters the Holy Place, he will bear the names of the sons of Israel *over his heart on the breastpiece of decision* as a continuing memorial before the LORD. (Exodus 28:29) (emphasis added)

One of the most important pieces of clothing the high priest wore was the breastplate or breastpiece. It was crafted with the same colors of gold, blue, purple, and scarlet as the ephod, representing the full nature of Jesus. On the breastplate were twelve stones inscribed with the twelve tribes of Israel, each listed by name. This demonstrates the intimate relationship the high priest had with the nation. Symbolically, this pointed to the great high priest, Jesus, who knows us individually by name: "The watchman opens the gate for him, and the sheep listen to his voice. He calls his own sheep by *name* and leads them out" (John 10:3; emphasis added).

On the ephod, Israel was represented on the high priest's shoulders. On the breastplate, the precious stones were placed close to the heart of the high priest. This placement demonstrated the tender affection and love the high priest had for the nation. When he interceded for the nation, he did it with strength and love. Jesus, our high priest, represents us today with strength and love: "But God demonstrates his own love for us in this: while we were still sinners, *Christ died for us*" (Romans 5:8) and "My dear children, I write this to you so that you will not sin. But if anybody does sin, we have *one who speaks to the Father in our defense*—Jesus Christ, the Righteous One" (1 John 2:1). (emphasis added)

He Wore a Linen Turban

> Make a plate of pure gold and engrave on it as on a seal: HOLY TO THE LORD. Fasten a blue cord to it to attach it to *the turban*; it is to be on the front of the turban. It will be on Aaron's forehead, and he will bear the guilt involved in the sacred gifts the Israelites consecrate, whatever their gifts may be. It will be on Aaron's forehead continually so that they will be acceptable to the Lord. (Exodus 28:36–38)

> Weave the tunic of fine linen and make the *turban of fine linen*. The sash is to be the work of an embroiderer. (Exodus 28:39) (emphasis added)

There is a tremendous picture of Christ in the turban. It was made of fine linen, again emphasizing the purity of the high priest. On the turban was placed a gold plate inscribed with the words: *Holy to the Lord*. The high priest was considered holy and set apart for the work of spiritual service. Because of this, he could present sacrifices for the sins of Israel. This action foreshadowed Jesus, who could represent us because the Father deemed Him worthy and holy. When Jesus was baptized, the Father declared that He was *well pleased* with Him. The Bible depicts Jesus to be holy and worthy of all praise: "The angel answered, 'The Holy Spirit will come upon you, and the power of the Most High will overshadow you. So the *holy one* to be born will be called the Son of God.'" (Luke 1:35) and "And they sang a new song: '*You are worthy* to take the scroll and to open its seals, because you were slain, and with your blood you purchased men for God'" (Revelation 5:9). (emphasis added)

He Wore a Waistband/Girdle

"Its skillfully woven *waistband* [translated *girdle* in the KJV] is to be like it—of one piece with the ephod and made with *gold*, and with *blue, purple* and *scarlet* yarn, and with *finely twisted linen*" (Exodus 28:8; emphasis added).

Servants, in the performance of their duties, commonly wore a waistband or girdle. The high priest was no different.

This waistband or girdle was designed to keep the ephod close to the body. Like many of the other pieces of clothing, it was made to reflect the colors of royalty and of humanity. The high priest stood between man and God while functioning as a servant of both. The girdle, in the form of a towel around the waist, was the item of clothing that Jesus took off when He washed the disciples' feet in John chapter 13. This was the ultimate picture of servanthood: "So he got up from the meal, took off his outer clothing, and wrapped a *towel around his waist*" (John 13:4; emphasis added).

Jesus serves us today by representing us before the Father: "For there is one God and one *mediator between God and men,* the man Christ Jesus" (1 Timothy 2:5; emphasis added).

The high priest's clothing foreshadows Christ in every detail. Everything pointed to that one perfect high priest, who would offer the ultimate sacrifice: His own body.

What Was His Main Function?

The main function of the high priest was to represent man before God in offering sacrifices for sin. The book of Hebrews makes this point clear: "Every high priest is selected from among men and is appointed to *represent them* in matters related to God, to offer gifts and sacrifices for sins" (Hebrews 5:1; emphasis added).

The high priest was in charge of this whole operation. However, there was one sacrifice that only he could perform. This was the sacrifice on the Day of Atonement. We will cover the Day of Atonement in the next chapter.

The High Priest of Israel in His Robes
of Glory and Beauty

DISCUSSION QUESTIONS

1. What was the importance of the linen clothes to the high priest? How does this apply to Jesus and to us?
2. The names of the sons of Israel appear on the ephod and the breastplate of the high priest. Explain the importance of the positioning of both as it related to the work of the high priest. How does this apply to Jesus?
3. What piece of the high priest's clothing did Jesus take off in John 13? Why was this important, and what are some practical ways we can demonstrate this function of servanthood?
4. What spiritual principle for New Testament believers does the relationship of the bells and the pomegranates located at the bottom of the high priest's robe illustrate?

14

The Day of Atonement

The Day of Atonement (Yom Kippur as it is commonly known) was the most important day in the calendar of Israel. On this hallowed occasion, the sins of the entire nation were atoned for on the mercy seat. The high priest's duties on the Day of Atonement postponed God's judgment on the nation for another year. God gave Moses meticulously detailed instructions for this special day. These orders were to be followed without a flaw, lest the nation be judged and the high priest killed. This sacred day would portend a time in the future when Jesus Himself would enact the Day of Atonement on the cross. Every action of the high priest symbolized this.

Step 1: Washes Himself and Dresses for Service

As the high priest commenced the procedures on the Day of Atonement, he did not initially wear his glorious garments, but the plain, ordinary linen garments. He first had to cleanse himself, emphasizing the purity of the high priest: "He is to put on the *sacred linen tunic, with linen undergarments* next to his body; he is to tie the linen sash around him and put on the linen turban. These are sacred garments; so he must bathe himself with water before he puts them on" (Leviticus 16:4; emphasis added).

In wearing plain linen garments, the focus was on his ordinary work and not his splendor. These points are important because, metaphorically speaking, when Jesus went to the cross, He was not dressed in beautiful garments. He looked like an ordinary man. He didn't adorn His glorious garments until later. Philippians underscores this aspect of Jesus' ministry: "Who, being in very nature God, did not consider equality with God something to be grasped, but made himself nothing, taking the very nature of a servant, *being made in human likeness. And being found in appearance as a man,* he humbled himself and became obedient to death—even death on a cross!" (Philippians 2:6–8; emphasis added).

This initial stage of the Day of Atonement was not for pomp and celebration. It was preparatory for dealing with the sins of the high priest and the people.

Step 2: Makes a Sin Offering for Himself

The Old Testament high priest was flawed and sinful. Therefore, he had to offer a sacrifice on the bronze altar for his own sin before he could perform this for the nation.

> Aaron shall bring the *bull* for *his own sin* offering to make atonement for himself and his household, and he is to slaughter the bull for his own sin offering. (Leviticus 16:11)

> But only the High Priest entered the inner room, and that only once a year, and never without blood, which *he offered for himself* and for the sins the people had committed in ignorance. (Hebrews 9:7) (emphasis added)

The bull was the animal used for the sin offering. The sin offering was considered the most detestable and repugnant of all the Old Testament offerings: "But the hide of the *bull* and all its flesh, as well as the head and legs, the inner parts and offal—that is, all the rest of the bull—he must take *outside the camp* to a place ceremonially clean, where the ashes are thrown, and burn it in a wood fire on the ash heap" (Leviticus 4:11–12; emphasis added).

A perfect high priest, Jesus Christ, would replace the imperfect one. Once the high priest offered a sacrifice on the bronze altar for his own sins, he was then ready for the next step. "Unlike the other high priests, *he does not need to offer sacrifices day after day, first for his own sins*, and then for the sins of the people. He sacrificed for their sins once for all when he offered himself" (Hebrews 7:27; emphasis added).

Step 3: Enters the Holy of Holies with Incense

> He is to take a censer *full of burning coals from the altar before the* LORD and two handfuls of finely ground fragrant incense and take them *behind the curtain.* He is to put the incense on the fire before the LORD, and the smoke of the incense will conceal the atonement cover above the Testimony, so that he will not die. (Leviticus 16:12–13; emphasis added)

Once he had sacrificed the bull on the altar of sacrifice in the courtyard, he proceeded into the holy place where the altar of incense was located. Then, he was to take coals off the altar and mix the fire with incense. Incense will now pervade the holy of holies, creating an aura of holiness and concealment of the mercy seat. This step also kept him from dying. Jesus, our high priest, did not have to do this. He was the perfect high priest: "For the law appoints as high priests men who are weak; but the oath, which came after the law, appointed the Son, who has been *made perfect* forever" (Hebrews 7:28; emphasis added).

Step 4: Puts the Blood of the Bull on the Mercy Seat

Upon entering the holy of holies, the high priest then places the blood on the mercy seat to atone for his own sins. "He is to take some of the bull's blood and with his finger sprinkle it on the front of the atonement cover; then *he shall sprinkle some of it with his finger seven times before the atonement cover*" (Leviticus 16:14; emphasis added).

He did this seven times. Seven is the perfect number. Again, Jesus did not have to do this for Himself when He placed His blood on the mercy seat of heaven.

Step 5: Makes a Sin Offering (First Goat) for the Nation

Now that the high priest has successfully atoned for his own sins, he was ready to atone for the sins of the nation. The whole process now had to be repeated, starting at the Altar of Sacrifice:

> He shall then *slaughter the goat* for the sin offering for the people and take its blood behind the curtain and do with it as he did with the bull's blood: He shall sprinkle it on the atonement cover and in front of it. In this way he will make atonement for the Most Holy Place because of the uncleanness and rebellion of the Israelites, whatever their sins have been. He is to do the same for the Tent of Meeting, which is among them in the midst of their uncleanness. (Leviticus 16:15–16; emphasis added)

The animal used to be the sin bearer for this offering, representing the nation, was the first of two goats. Remember, the goatskin was one of the hides used to cover the tabernacle proper. The high priest took the blood of the goat through the holy place and into the holy of holies. He then repeated what he had already done for his own sins; he sprinkled the blood on the mercy seat seven times. The book of Hebrews paints a poignant picture of Jesus performing these acts as well: "He did not enter by means of the blood of *goats* and *calves*; but *he entered the Most Holy Place once for all by his own blood*, having obtained eternal redemption" (Hebrews 9:12; emphasis added).

Step 6: Blood is Sprinkled on the Altar of Incense

After the high priest placed the goat's blood on the mercy seat, he then went back into the holy place, where he sprinkled the blood of the bull (representing his own sin) and the blood of the goat (representing the sins of the nation) on the altar of incense. This symbolized God's acceptance of the offering and His willingness to withhold judgment on the people for one year. This was not a permanent solution for sin because this procedure would have to be done all over again the next year:

> *Once a year* Aaron shall make atonement on its horns. This *annual atonement* must be made with the blood of the atoning sin offering for the generations to come. It is most holy to the LORD. (Exodus 30:10)

> Then he shall come out to the altar that is before the LORD and make atonement for it. He shall take some of the *bull's blood and some of the goat's blood* and put it on all the horns of the altar. He shall sprinkle some of the blood on it with his finger seven times to cleanse it and to consecrate it from the uncleanness of the Israelites. (Leviticus 16:18–19) (emphasis added)

Step 7: The Scapegoat (Second Goat) was Sent Away

Earlier, we mentioned that there were two goats involved in the process on the Day of Atonement. The first goat was slain for the sins of the people, and its blood placed on the mercy seat. However, the second goat represented a more pleasurable task:

> When Aaron has finished making atonement for the Most Holy Place, the Tent of Meeting and the altar, he shall bring forward the *live goat*. He is to lay both hands on the head of the live goat and confess over it all the wickedness and rebellion of the Israelites—all their sins—and put them on the goat's head. He shall *send the goat away* into the desert in the care of a man appointed for the task. The goat will *carry on itself all their sins* to a solitary place; and the man shall release it in the desert. (Leviticus 16:20–22; emphasis added)

Whereas the first goat was the payment for the sin and had to die, the second goat took the sin away and lived. The high priest placed his hands on the live goat and transferred the sins of the nation on to it. The goat was then sent away, illustrating the fact that the sins of the nation had been taken away. This is where the common term in our day *scapegoat* is derived. The goat escaped with the sins of the nation. Whereas the first goat pictured death, paying for the sins of the people, the second goat pictured resurrection and life, taking the sins away. This is an incredible symbol of what Jesus Christ would do to accomplish our salvation. It took the death of Christ as well as the resurrection of Christ to secure forgiveness of sin and complete the process of redemption: "And if Christ has not been raised, our preaching is *useless* and so is your faith" (1 Corinthians 15:14; emphasis added).

When John the Baptist saw Jesus, he declared Him as the one who takes sin away: "The next day John saw Jesus coming toward him and said, 'Look, the Lamb of God, who *takes away the sin* of the world!'" (John 1:29; emphasis added).

Remember, those outside the tabernacle could not see this process. However, when they saw the goat run away, they knew the atonement for their sins was complete, and the nation could rest for another year.

Step 8: Puts on His Glorious Garments

At this point, the high priest went back into the holy place and put on his beautiful garments again: "Then Aaron is to go into the Tent of Meeting and take off the linen garments he put on before he entered the Most Holy Place, and he is to leave them there. He shall bathe himself with water in a holy place and *put on his regular garments*" (Leviticus 16:23–24; emphasis added).

This is where the bells at the bottom of the high priest's robe once again came into importance. If the people did not hear the bells, they knew that the high priest was dead. However, if they heard the bells, they were assured he was alive. The people did not rejoice at their forgiveness until they were certain that the high priest survived.

Remember, during the atonement process, the priest wore ordinary clothes. He was not allowed to adorn the attractive garments until the atonement process was completed. This was also true of Jesus. He laid down His heavenly garments until after He had insured our salvation.

Before Salvation: Plain Garments

Paul eloquently and powerfully describes what it meant for the Son of God to come to earth, divest himself of heavenly expressions, and take on the appearance of a human being. He was even willing to die an ignoble and common death: "Who, being in very nature God, did not consider equality with God something to be grasped, but made himself nothing, taking the *very nature of a servant, being made in human likeness.* And being *found in appearance as a man*, he humbled himself and became obedient to death—even death on a cross!" (Philippians 2:6–8; emphasis added).

Jesus was willing to live an ordinary and unspectacular life on earth. Much like the high priest of the Old Testament, He wore the ordinary garments.

After Salvation: Glorious Garments

In the book of Revelation, we behold this same high priest in different garments: glorious ones. Up to this point, John had only seen Jesus in his earthly, plain garments; now he beholds Him dressed in a regal and spectacular fashion: "I turned around to see the voice that was speaking to me. And when I turned I saw seven golden lampstands, and among the lampstands was someone 'like a son of man,' *dressed in a robe reaching down to his feet and with a golden sash around his chest*" (Revelation 1:12–13; emphasis added).

In this passage, the Son of Man is dressed in wonderful, beautiful clothes. These are the clothes that now adorn Him because the work of atonement has been accomplished. In this way, He fulfills the symbol of the high priest in the Old Testament by wearing his glorious attire.

Step 9: Offers a Burnt Offering

After putting on his glorious garments, the high priest proceeded to offer a burnt offering unto the Lord. "Then he shall come out and sacrifice the *burnt offering* for himself and the burnt offering for the people, to make atonement for himself and for the people" (Leviticus 16:24; emphasis added).

The burnt offering symbolized two things: that which was pleasing to the Lord, and that which was totally given over to the Lord for service. In essence, the high priest was offering the nation to the Lord for His purposes. This offering had a sweet aroma associated with it, indicating its pleasantness to the Lord. The entire animal was burned in this sacrifice, demonstrating that which is totally surrendered to God. Ultimately, this process pictured Jesus's supreme sacrifice, which was pleasing and acceptable to His Father. The New Testament confirms this: "And live a life of love, just as Christ loved us and gave himself up for us as a *fragrant* offering and sacrifice to God" (Ephesians 5:2; emphasis added).

Jesus was not only acceptable to the Father, but He made us acceptable to Him as well. The burnt offering is symbolic of the giving of our lives for the Lord's service. In the New Testament, whenever we see the words *aroma*, *fragrant*, *pleasing*, or *living sacrifice*, we know that these are references to the burnt offering. Paul references the giving of our lives as a burnt offering in his epistle: "Therefore, I urge you, brothers, in view of God's mercy, to offer your bodies as *living sacrifices*, holy and *pleasing* to God—this is your spiritual act of worship" (Romans 12:1; emphasis added).

Step 10: Sin Bearers' Carcasses are Burned Outside the Camp

Up to this point, two animals have been slain: the bull was sacrificed for the sins of the high priest, and the first goat for the sins of the people. Now, in further symbolism, their wretched carcasses must be eliminated: "The bull and the goat for the sin offerings, whose blood was brought into the Most Holy Place to make atonement, must be taken *outside the camp*; their hides, flesh and offal are to be *burned up*" (Leviticus 16:27–28; emphasis added).

The remains of the sacrificial goat and bull were to be totally burned outside the camp of Israel. They were considered repugnant and detestable as the animals sacrificed for the sins and guilt of the high priest and nation. The writer of Hebrews demonstrates that this Old Testament act, was ultimately a shadow and type of what would eventually happen to Jesus on the cross:

"The high priest carries the blood of animals into the Most Holy Place as a sin offering, but the bodies are burned outside the camp. And so Jesus also suffered *outside the city* gate to make the people holy through his own blood" (Hebrews 13:11–12; emphasis added).

Jesus's was crucified outside the temple and outside the city of Jerusalem. His body was disgraced and savaged. He was mocked by the Jews and the Romans. Jesus even indicates on the cross that His Father had to turn away because of the sin laid upon him: "About the ninth hour Jesus cried out in a loud voice, 'Eloi, Eloi, lama sabachthani?' —which means, *My God, my God, why have you forsaken me?*'" (Matthew 27:46; emphasis added).

But in the end, all of this shame turned to victory and glory as Jesus rose from the dead and secured salvation for all who would believe.

The Process Was Effective for One Year

The problem with the Old Testament Day of Atonement was that it was incapable of permanently dealing with the sin issue. The rituals and ceremonies on this important day were to be practiced every year: "This is to be a lasting ordinance for you: atonement is to be made *once a year* for all the sins of the Israelites. And it was done, as the LORD commanded Moses" Leviticus 16:34; emphasis added).

Israel had no guarantee their sins would be atoned for on a permanent basis. The tabernacle system was a temporary solution to the sin problem until someone could come along and make it permanent. This person was Jesus Christ. He became the final sacrifice who could once and for all bring permanent certainty of the forgiveness for sin:

> He did not enter by means of the blood of goats and calves; but he entered the Most Holy Place *once for all* by his own blood, having obtained eternal redemption...How much more, then, will the blood of Christ, who through the eternal Spirit offered himself unblemished to God, cleanse our consciences from acts that lead to death, so that we may serve the living God! (Hebrews 9:12,14; emphasis added)

DISCUSSION QUESTIONS

1. What step on the Day of Atonement did Jesus not have to perform? Support your point with scripture. What are the implications of this for the church?
2. Explain the symbolic meaning of the two goats and how they relate to our salvation.
3. Why did the high priest begin the Day of Atonement process in his linen garments but end the day in his glorious garments? How does this picture Christ?
4. What is the main important difference between the Day of Atonement in the Old Testament, and what Christ performed in the New Testament? Why is this essential to the message of Christianity?

15

Key Offerings Under the Law

The tabernacle was a complex system of religious activity, sacrifices, and offerings. The people offered many sacrifices continually to Jehovah throughout the year. Each offering was a symbolic type of some aspect of our Christian life.

Sin Offering: The Penalty for Sin

As you recall, a sin offering was performed once a year during the Day of Atonement. But this offering was also offered during the year when sins were committed:

> The Lord said to Moses, "Say to Aaron and his sons: 'These are the regulations for the *sin offering*: The *sin offering* is to be slaughtered before the Lord in the place the burnt offering is slaughtered; it is most holy.'" (Leviticus 6:24)

> Say to the Israelites: "When anyone sins unintentionally and does what is forbidden in any of the Lord's commands. If the anointed priest sins, bringing guilt on the people, he must bring to the Lord a young bull without defect as a *sin offering* for the sin he has committed…But the hide of the bull and all its flesh, as well as the head and legs, the inner parts and offal—that is, all the rest of the bull—he must take outside the camp to a place ceremonially clean, where the ashes are thrown, and burn it in a wood fire on the ash heap." (Leviticus 4:2–3, 11–12) (emphasis added)

The sin offering was made for sins in general. In most cases, a bull was used although other animals were utilized in some situations. This sacrifice focused on the penalty for sin and was considered shameful and repugnant. The remaining parts of the bull were to be taken outside the camp because they were viewed as despicable. This offering corresponds with Christ's taking our sin upon Himself and being killed outside the temple:

> God made him who had no sin *to be sin for us*, so that in him we might become the righteousness of God. (2 Corinthians 5:21)

> The High Priest carries the blood of animals into the Most Holy Place as a sin offering, but the bodies are burned outside the camp. And so Jesus also suffered *outside the city gate* to make the people holy through his own blood. (Hebrews 13:11–12)

> *He himself bore our sins* in his body on the tree, so that we might die to sins and live for righteousness; by his wounds you have been healed. (1 Peter 2:24) (emphasis added)

Guilt Offering: Daily Sins

Whereas the sin offering was given for sins in general, the guilt offering was to be done for specific sins. Notice in the following verses, the guilt offering highlights the person or individual and demands restitution, focusing on the specific nature of the sin:

> The LORD said to Moses: "When a *person* commits a violation and sins unintentionally in regard to any of the Lord's holy things, he is to bring to the LORD as a penalty a ram from the flock, one without defect and of the proper value in silver, according to the sanctuary shekel. It is a *guilt offering*. He must *make restitution* for what he has failed to do in regard to the holy things, add a fifth of the value to that and give it all to the priest, who will make atonement for

him with the ram as a *guilt offering*, and he will be forgiven." (Leviticus 5:14–16; emphasis added)

The sin offering was more detestable and had greater shame associated with it, but this offering seems less harsh. The bull was the animal of choice for the sin offering while the ram was the animal selected for the guilt offering. The guilt offering symbolizes our need for daily cleansing from sin and our need to have specific sins forgiven. Also, it focused more on the restoration of the sinner in his daily practice. This is what Jesus was referring to during the Last Supper with His disciples: "Jesus answered, 'A person who has had a bath needs only to wash his feet; his whole body is clean. And you are clean, though not every one of you.'" (John 13:10; emphasis added).

Other New Testament writers speak of this need for cleansing of specific sins: "Therefore confess your sins to each other and pray for each other so that you may be healed. The prayer of a righteous man is powerful and effective" (James 5:16) and "If we claim to be without sin, we deceive ourselves and the truth is not in us. If we confess our sins, He is faithful and just and will forgive us our sins and purify us from all unrighteousness" (1 John 1:8–9).

Some older translations refer to the guilt offering as the trespass offering.

Burnt Offering: Committed Life

The burnt offering was a special, positive sacrifice. It was also known as the sweet, fragrant offering.

> The LORD called to Moses and spoke to him from the Tent of Meeting. He said, "Speak to the Israelites and say to them: 'When any of you brings an offering to the LORD, bring as your offering an animal from either the herd or the flock. If the offering is a *burnt offering* from the herd, he is to offer a male without defect. He must present it at the entrance to the Tent of Meeting so that it will be acceptable to the

LORD. He is to lay his hand on the head of the *burnt offering*, and it will be accepted on his behalf to make atonement for him. He is to wash the inner parts and the legs with water, and the priest is to burn all of it on the altar. It is a *burnt offering*, an offering made by fire, an *aroma pleasing* to the LORD.'" (Leviticus 1:1–4, 9; emphasis added)

The animal used in the burnt offering could have no defect, and the entire animal had to be consumed by the fire. It was a pleasing offering, which signified the total surrender of one's life to God. Whenever the burnt offering is referred to in the New Testament, the focus is on commitment of life. The New Testament makes several references to this offering by using words like *acceptable*, *pleasing*, and *fragrant*:

Therefore, I urge you, brothers, in view of God's mercy, to offer your bodies as living *sacrifices*, holy and *pleasing* to God—this is your spiritual act of worship. (Romans 12:1)

To be a minister of Christ Jesus to the Gentiles with the priestly duty of proclaiming the gospel of God, so that the Gentiles might become an *offering acceptable* to God, sanctified by the Holy Spirit. (Romans 15:16)

I have received full payment and even more; I am amply supplied, now that I have received from Epaphroditus the gifts you sent. They are a *fragrant offering*, an *acceptable sacrifice, pleasing* to God. (Philippians 4:18)

And live a life of love, just as Christ loved us and gave himself up for us as a *fragrant offering and sacrifice* to God. (Ephesians 5:2)

Therefore, since we are receiving a kingdom that cannot be shaken, let us be thankful, and so worship God *acceptably* with reverence and awe, for our God is a *consuming fire*. (Hebrews 12:28–29) (emphasis added)

The Hebrews 12:28–29 passage is interesting because it depicts God as a consuming fire. Remember, the burnt offering was to be totally consumed by fire. The writer is exhorting us to offer God the kind of sacrifice (burnt offering) that He would consume and be totally pleased with. Romans 12:1–2 is literally a commentary on the burnt offering. For a full discussion of this, please see my book *Christianity is a White Collar Job.*

Grain Offering: Purity of Life

The grain offering was unique in that it did not directly require the shedding of blood. However, it was very closely associated with the burnt offering, which did require the blood sacrifice of an animal. The two main components in the grain offering were oil and fine flour:

> When someone brings a *grain offering* to the LORD, his offering is to be of fine flour. He is to pour *oil* on it, put incense on it and take it to Aaron's sons the priests. The priest shall take a handful of the *fine flour and oil*, together with all the incense, and burn this as a memorial portion on the altar, an offering made by fire, an aroma pleasing to the LORD. The rest of the grain offering belongs to Aaron and his sons; it is a most holy part of the offerings made to the LORD by fire. (Leviticus 2:1–3) (emphasis added)

This offering reflects our devotion to God and willingness to be led by the Spirit, which is symbolized by the oil. The flour was to have no yeast or impurity. Again, this sacrifice focused on one's willingness to lead a pure and holy life in daily fellowship with the Lord. It was also called the meal offering and was presented in conjunction with the burnt offering. The New Testament supports these ideas:

> The Spirit of the Lord is on me. (Luke 4:18)

"My food," said Jesus, "is to do the will of him who sent me and to finish his work." (John 4:34)

The one who sent me is with me; he has not left me alone, for I always do what pleases him. (John 8:29)

Drink Offering: Ultimate Sacrifice

Like the grain offering, the drink offering was presented in conjunction with the burnt offering: blood was the foundation for it. At the very last part of the ceremony, the worshiper would pour a cup of wine on the burnt offering.

> Together with its grain offering of two-tenths of an ephah of fine flour mixed with oil—an offering made to the LORD by fire, a pleasing aroma—and its *drink offering* of a quarter of a hin of wine. (Leviticus 23:13)

> Also bring half a hin of wine as a *drink offering*. It will be an offering made by fire, an aroma pleasing to the LORD. (Numbers 15:10) (emphasis added)

The wine offering was a special touch that went beyond the normal burnt offering. In the New Testament, it pictured the ultimate devotion to God: the sacrifice of our lives. Paul alluded to this offering when he referred to his martyr's death: "But even if I am being poured out like a *drink offering* on the sacrifice and service coming from your faith, I am glad and rejoice with all of you" (Philippians 2:17) and "For I am already being poured out like a *drink offering*, and the time has come for my departure" (2 Timothy 4:6). (emphasis added)

Physical death is the ultimate sacrifice one can offer the Lord. This is true of all martyrs and those who have laid their lives on the line for the cause of Christ.

Fellowship Offering: Communion with God

The fellowship offering was also referred to as the peace offering.

> If someone's offering is a *fellowship offering*, and he offers an animal from the herd, whether male or female, he is to present before the LORD an animal without defect. He is to lay his hand on the head of his offering and slaughter it at the entrance to the Tent of Meeting. Then Aaron's sons the priests shall sprinkle the blood against the altar on all sides. From the fellowship offering he is to bring a sacrifice made to the LORD by fire: all the fat that covers the inner parts or is connected to them. (Leviticus 3:1–3)

> The meat of his *fellowship offering* of thanksgiving must be eaten on the day it is offered; he must leave none of it till morning. (Leviticus 7:15) (emphasis added)

This was the only offering from which the worshiper could eat, underscoring his fellowship, communion, and peace with God. The priest could also partake of this offering. The New Testament exhorts us to have fellowship with God because we have peace with Him and are no longer enemies:

> Therefore, since we have been justified through faith, we have *peace* with God through our Lord Jesus Christ. (Romans 5:1)

> But now in Christ Jesus you who once were far away have been brought near through the blood of Christ. For *he himself is our peace*, who has made the two one and has destroyed the barrier, the dividing wall of hostility. (Ephesians 2:13–14)

> If we claim to have *fellowship with him* yet walk in the darkness, we lie and do not live by the truth. But if we walk in the light, as He is in the light, we have fellowship with one another, and the blood of Jesus, his Son, purifies us from all sin. (1 John 1:6–7) (emphasis added)

Each of these offerings illustrates some aspect of the believer's relationship with God. Christ has removed our guilt and allowed us to live in fellowship with and in consecration to God. Because our sins are forgiven, we now have the freedom to enjoy God forever.

Offering Meaning Fulfillment

Sin offering	Penalty of sin	1 Peter 2:24
Guilt offering	Daily sins	1 John 1:8–9
Burnt offering	Committed life	Romans 12:1
Grain offering	Purity of life	John 8:29
Drink offering	Ultimate sacrifice	Phil 2:17; 2 Tim 4:6
Fellowship offering	Communion with God	1 John 1:6–7

DISCUSSION QUESTIONS

1. What was the main function of the burnt offering? In Romans 12:1–2, find the similarities to the burnt offering in the Old Testament.
2. What do the two ingredients of the grain offering symbolize for the Christian life?
3. Where does the drink offering appear in the New Testament? What is the drink offering's essential meaning? Can you give an example of someone in modern times who has offered a drink offering to the Lord?
4. What does it mean to be at peace with God? What scriptures from the New Testament illustrate this?

Conclusion

The tabernacle is the Bible's most important symbol of grace and mercy in the Old Testament. It is a clarion salvation message, culminating in the death and resurrection of Christ. Many Old Testament, as well as New Testament, books make direct or tacit references to this wonderful tent.

Revelation and the Tabernacle

No New Testament book emphasizes the tabernacle more than the book of Revelation. After Jesus appears to John clothed in His glorious garments in Revelation 1, in chapters 4 and 5, He opens up the heavens to His old friend and shows him the magnificence and power of the throne of God. There are numerous references to the tabernacle in these two chapters as well as the rest of the book. This brings us assurance that the tabernacle Moses saw in heaven thousands of years ago is still active and influencing planet earth today. Here are some of the tabernacle references in Revelation 4 and 5:

Holy of Holies and the Glory of God

"At once I was in the Spirit, and there before me was a throne in heaven *with someone sitting on it*" (Revelation 4:2; emphasis added).

Revelation introduces us to a throne with someone sitting on it. This obviously is a reference to the presence and glory of God the Father. The holy of holies contained the presence of God.

Lampstands/Seven Lamps

"From the throne came flashes of lightning, rumblings and peals of thunder. Before the throne, *seven lamps* were blazing. These are the seven spirits of God" (Revelation 4:5; emphasis added). We noted that the lampstand in the holy place contained a total of seven lamps. In heaven, this light emanates from the seven lamps, which are the seven spirits of God.

Cherubim/Four Living Creatures

> The first *living creature* was like a lion, the second was like an ox, the third had a face like a man, the fourth was like a flying eagle. Each of the four *living creatures* had six wings and was covered with eyes all around, even under his wings. Day and night they never stop saying: "Holy, holy, holy is the Lord God Almighty, who was, and is, and is to come." (Revelation 4:6–8; emphasis added)

The cherubim were the majestic angelic beings who were an integral part of the fabric in the veil, as well as the atonement cover on the mercy seat. They were defenders of the holiness of God and executers of God's righteousness and justice.

In Revelation 6:1–7, when God's wrath is apparent, the cherubim focus on the holiness of God. These cherubim appear as four animals: the eagle (mightiest among the birds), the bull (mightiest among domestic animals), the lion (mightiest among the wild animals), and man (mightiest of them all). All that is noblest, strongest, wisest, and swiftest in animate nature is represented at the throne of God. This again is something we see in the Old Testament, particularly in the Book of Ezekiel: "These were the living creatures I had seen beneath the God of Israel by the Kebar River and I realized that they were *cherubim*" (Ezekiel 10:20; emphasis added).

In keeping with their designed function, these creatures cry, "Holy, holy, holy." This triple use of the Greek word for holy, *hagios*, is called a Trisagion. It is used only here and in Isaiah 6:3. In the scriptures, holiness is the only attribute of God mentioned in this threefold emphasis. God is absolutely separate from all of creation, and He is to be respected as holy.

Bronze Altar of Sacrifice/Slain Lamb

"Then I saw a *Lamb*, looking as if it had *been slain*, standing in the center of the throne, encircled by the four living creatures and the elders. He had seven horns and seven eyes, which are the seven spirits of God sent out into all the earth" (Revelation 5:6; emphasis added).

The bronze altar of sacrifice in the Old Testament tabernacle was where the animals were slain by the priest (Exodus 27:1–8 and Leviticus 1:8). Although not directly mentioned, its presence is subtly implied as John sees the Lamb of God in the heavenly tabernacle as the sacrificial animal freshly slain.

Mercy Seat/Jesus's blood

"And they sang a new song: 'You are worthy to take the scroll and to open its seals, because you were slain, and *with your blood* you *purchased men* for God from every tribe and language and people and nation'" (Revelation 5:9; emphasis added).

The mercy seat, which sat on top of the Ark of the Covenant is where the blood was spread to atone for sins (Exodus 25:17–21 and 30:10). In this verse, we witness the blood of Jesus purchasing the redeemed. Christ has become the mercy seat.

Altar of Incense

And when he had taken it, the four living creatures and the twenty-four elders fell down before the Lamb. Each one had a harp and they were holding *golden bowls full of incense, which are the prayers of the saints.* (Revelation 5:8)

Another angel, who had a golden censer, came and stood at the altar. He was given much incense to offer, with the prayers of all the saints, on the *golden altar* before the throne. The smoke of the incense, together with the prayers of the saints, went up before God from the angel's hand. Then the angel took the censer, filled it with fire from *the altar*, and hurled it on the earth; and there came peals of thunder, rumblings, flashes of lightning and an earthquake. (Revelation 8:3–5) (emphasis added)

The altar of incense represented the worship and prayers of the saints in the tabernacle (Exodus 30:1–6). In Revelation, we see the real live worship and prayers of the saints working effectually at the throne. The word *altar* is even mentioned in Revelation 8.

High Priest

"*He came* and took the scroll from the right hand of him who sat on the throne" (Revelation 5:7; emphasis added).

The high priest in the Old Testament had to offer sacrifices annually for his sins and for the sins of the people (Leviticus 16:11–16). He was the highest ranking spiritual leader in Israel. Though imperfect, he foreshadowed another high priest who would come later in perfection and procure salvation and establish His authority in the world. In this verse, Jesus, the perfect high priest, receives the mantle of authority to rule in the earth.

This cosmic tabernacle is placed strategically in chapters 4 and 5 to set the tone for the rest of the book. In the Old Testament, the tabernacle was the center of God's operations on the earth. It symbolized His presence, power, and plan of salvation for mankind. In the New Testament, God's heavenly tabernacle is also operational on the earth in a greater way than it was in the Old Testament. The tabernacles of Moses and David have long since passed, but the tabernacle in heaven is still functioning powerfully on the earth. God is in control, and the Lamb is worthy to be praised.

Summarizing the Tabernacle of Grace

The study of the Old Testament tabernacle is truly a view of God's wonderful and gracious plan of salvation for a sinful people. While many see the God of the Old Testament as harsh, judgmental, cruel, ruthless, and mean, the tabernacle is a giant beacon demonstrating the grace, love, and forgiveness of God. Here is a summary of some of the great themes the tabernacle teaches us:

- Salvation is God's idea. It never originates with man.
- God's grace and mercy are big enough to cover all of man's sinfulness.
- The Old Testament tabernacle was temporary and imperfect but foreshadowed a permanent and perfect salvation plan provided by Christ, through His death and resurrection.
- The simple and plain nature of the tabernacle pictured that salvation would come in the form of an "ordinary man": Jesus Christ.
- Man is inherently sinful and must have Christ in his life to be whole.
- Worship of God is reserved for those who have been washed by the blood of Christ.
- The tabernacle was where man met God, guilt met grace, and sin met forgiveness.
- Salvation is not only about the forgiveness of sins but a communal life with God for those who know Him.
- The veil blocking the entrance into the throne of God has been torn, and now, followers of Christ can boldly enter into His presence.
- God will always have a tabernacle on the earth. The tabernacle today is the church of Jesus Christ. Like the priests of the Old Testament, we, the New Testament priests, transport God's glory and salvation plan to the world.
- Christ is the *only* true light and pathway to God. He is the *only* way through which mankind's sins can be forgiven and salvation attained. The tabernacle is about God's grace manifested in the cross of Christ, not about human effort masked in human religion.

Scripture Index

38:25–27-79
40:34–37-152

Leviticus
1:1–4-189
1:8-60
2:1–3-191
3:1–3-193
4:2–3-187
4:11–12-176,187
5:14–16-188
6:12–13-62
6:24-187
7:15-193
9:24-61
10:1–2-120
16:4-175
16:11-176
16:12–13-62,177
16:14-146,177
16:15–16-146,178
16:18–22-83,179
16:23–24-180,182
16:27–28-183
16:34-183
23:13-192
24:5–6-105
24:7-109
24:8–9-104,106,108

Numbers
2:3-47
3:38-48
4:7-106
4:9-99
9:18–23-39
15:10-192
17:6–8-136
21:9-59

I Samuel
4:3–4-40
4:21-154
6:19-138
7:1–2-139

2 Samuel
6:6–7-139
6:13-140

1 Kings
8:9-137
6:19–20-155

I Chronicles
6:31–32-41

2 Chronicles
2:5–6-153
5:13–14-153

Psalm
18:10-145
23:5-112
51:10-70
119:9-70
141:2-118

Isaiah
6:1-27,98
53:2–6-35,60,84,95,97,145

Ezekiel
1:26–28-28
10:20-198
41:4-155
44:15–18-167

Daniel
7:9-28

Hosea
11:4-86

Amos
9:11–12-41

Haggai
1:2-3-153
1:9-153

Zecchariah
4:2, 4, 6-99

NEW TESTAMENT
Matthew
4:4-107
6:9–10-119
5:14–16-94,97
27:46-183
27:50–51-128
28:19–20-40,63

Mark
16:15-40

Luke
1:35-171
4:18-191
19:10-24
22:19-105
24:26–27-19,95
24:39-148

John
1:4–5-78,98
1:7-94
1:8–9-98
1:12-81
1:14-20,26,36,156
1:29-60,84,180

3:5–6-39
3:14–59
4:24-70
4:34-192
5:39-19
6:35-105,107
6:44–45-24
6:51-135
6:53-105
6:54-135
6:57–58-108
8:29-192
9:5-94
10:3-170
10:7-51
10:28-111
13:4-172
13:10-69,189
14:6-51
14:17-158
15:1–5-96,97
15:16-24
19:30-110
19:34-97
20:17-148

Acts
1:8-99
4:12-51,81,126
7:44-23
7:55–56-111
10:43-80
15:14–17-42
17:24-157
20:28-80

Romans
1:16-62
3:20-26
3:23–24-26

3:25-147
5:1-107,193
5:6-209
5:7-103
5:8-87,170
5:9-209
5:10-127
7:7-137
8:3–5-145
8:10–11-158
8:34-117
10:4-137
12:1-182,190
15:16-190

1 Corinthians
1:18-62
1:30-159
2:14–15-82
3:16-156
6:19-156
6:20-80
10:16–17-104,106
15:14, 17-136,180

2 Corinthians
3:6–9-26
3:10–13-152
3:18-157
4:6–7-85
5:1-20,60
5:14-80
5:18–21-22,63,126,144,156

Galatians
3:11-26
3:14-80
3:23–25-137
5:22-96

Ephesians
1:4-159
1:22–23-106
2:1–3-127
2:13–14-193
2:8–9-26
2:18-118
2:21–22-157
3:12-118
5:2-109,182,190
5:8–9-94,99
3:17–18-69
5:8–10-94
5:26-70
6:17-108

Philippians
2:6–8-22,78,85,175
2:17-192
4:18-190

Colossians
1:19-21
1:27-20,140,157
2:16-17-19

1 Thessalonians
1:10-144
5:9-62
5:17-121

1 Timothy
2:5-172

2 Timothy
3:16–17-107

Titus
3:5-39